Klett Lektürehilfen

Tom Franklin

Crooked Letter, Crooked Letter

Interpretationshilfe für Oberstufe und Abitur
in englischer Sprache

von
Sarah Nowotny

Klett Lerntraining

Sarah Nowotny kommt aus London und hat langjährige Erfahrung als Lehrerin. Sie ist als freie Autorin und Übersetzerin tätig.

Die Textzitate folgen der Ausgabe: Tom Franklin: Crooked Letter, Crooked Letter. London: Pan Macmillan, 2014 (12011).

Bibliografische Information der Deutschen Nationalbibliothek
Die Deutsche Nationalbibliothek verzeichnet diese Publikation in der Deutschen Nationalbibliografie; detaillierte bibliografische Daten sind im Internet über http://dnb.dnb.de abrufbar

4. Auflage 2020

www.klett-lerntraining.de
kundenservice@klett-lerntraining.de
Umschlagfoto: laif, Köln (Ulf ANDERSEN/GAMMA-RAPHO/laif)
Satz: DOPPELPUNKT, Stuttgart
Druck: medienhaus Plump GmbH, Rheinbreitbach
Printed in Germany
ISBN 978-3-12-923141-8

1 The Plot

2 Analysis and Interpretation

1 The Plot

Chapter One

INFO AT A GLANCE

An introduction to Larry Ott

- Larry is a loner who lives in isolation from the rest of society.
- He is suspected of having killed a girl.
- When he returns home one morning, a gunman in a mask is waiting for him and shoots him in the chest.

The novel opens with two attention-grabbing facts: a girl is missing and there is a monster waiting for Larry Ott at his house. It starts as an ordinary day for Larry, a forty-one year old single man who lives in his parents' house in the Mississippi countryside. It is an isolated place: his nearest neighbor lives a mile away and there are no shops nearby. On this particular morning, he goes about his usual activities, going out on his tractor to cut the grass and feeding his chickens. When his parents were still around, they had also had chickens, which had lived in a relatively small space at the side of the barn. Feeling sorry for the birds, Larry had constructed a movable cage which allowed him to take the chickens to different parts of his field when the weather was good. While getting food and water for the birds, he talks to them politely: "Have a good day, ladies" (P 4 / K 20)*, almost as if they are friends of his.

Dramatic opening grabs the reader's attention

Larry lives in isolation

Larry works as a mechanic, "but only in theory" (ibid.). He has a small workshop with space for two cars and an old pickup truck that had belonged to his father. He keeps tools in it in case he is called out to help someone whose car has broken down. There is a gun rack in the truck, but Larry uses it to hold his umbrella. He is not allowed to own a gun anyway, due to an incident in his past.

His business is unsuccessful

* This study guide contains quotations from two editions of *Crooked Letter, Crooked Letter*: the 2011 Pan Macmillan edition (P + page number) and the 2017 Klett edition (K + page number).

He knows he won't have any customers

Larry puts on his mechanic's uniform and makes himself breakfast, watching the news while he eats it. Once again, the missing girl is mentioned: she has not been found yet. He makes his way carefully through the mud to his truck and drives to work. He already knows what his working day will be like. He'll open up the shop and get everything ready for the day, hoping that, for once, he might have a customer. But, as usual, he will spend the day drinking Coke and reading at his desk.

Today, however, there is a change in Larry's usual routine. He gets a call from the nursing home where his mother now lives, telling him that she's having a good day and would like him to bring lunch for them to eat together. He decides to go home first to get a photo album, because looking at old photos helps his mother to remember who she is.

He usually drives carefully because he is under observation

Since he wants to get to the nursing home as quickly as possible, Larry drives fast, although he knows this is not a good idea. The police usually watch out for him, ready to catch him if he does something wrong. Apart from local teenagers, who sometimes come to his yard in the middle of the night to make a noise and throw beer bottles, and his one friend Wallace Stringfellow, Larry's only visitors are the police. One particular police officer, Roy French, comes to his house from time to time with a search warrant and goes over his property:

> "You understand, right," French always said, tapping him on the chest with the paper. "I got to explore every possibility. You're what we call a person of interest." (P 6 / K 22)

He understands why the police suspect him

Larry never resists these visits, but sits patiently on his porch until the search has been completed. He does understand why the police come, knowing that he is the kind of person who could be suspected of killing a girl: "If he'd been missing a daughter, he would come here too." (P 7 / K 23) He knows that the police have to search everywhere, even if they never find anything.

On this occasion, he gets a shock when he enters the house. A shoe box is lying open on the table, and when he turns he sees the face of a monster. Straight away, he knows that the person standing in his house is wearing a gray zombie mask that belongs to him, and that he had kept hidden in the shoe box. He realizes that this intruder has found something that French, the police officer, had never discovered. Before he can really start to speak, the man in the mask points a gun at him: "Ever body knows what you did." (Ibid.) Larry is defenseless. He wants to tell the man that he didn't kidnap either the Rutherford girl, who has been missing since last week, or a girl called Cindy Walker, who disappeared twenty-five years ago. However, he does not get the chance. The man pushes the gun into Larry's chest and, just before he fires it, Larry feels that he recognizes something about the man's eyes.

Up to now, Larry has managed to hide the mask from the police

The man shoots Larry in the chest

When Larry opens his eyes again, he is lying on the floor. His attacker is leaning against the wall, watching him. Breathing hard and visibly shaking, the gunman tells Larry to die. Although he is not in pain, Larry can feel the blood flowing from his chest. Looking over at his attacker, he feels only sympathy and forgiveness "because all monsters were misunderstood" (P 8 / K 24). The man in the mask has got Larry's blood on his clothes, and appears nervous, passing the gun from one hand to the other. Larry can hear a buzzing sound in his head. When his attacker once again tells him to die, he knows that he would be glad to do so.

Larry feels sympathy for his attacker

He is willing to die

Chapter Two

INFO AT A GLANCE

An introduction to Silas Jones

- Silas has returned to the small town where he grew up to work as a police constable.
- He knew Larry as a boy but has avoided him since returning to Chabot.
- It seems that the two of them share a secret.
- When he hears that Larry is not at work, he is sure something is wrong.

Silas Jones is the only police officer in the very small town of Chabot, Mississippi. He is seldom called by his real name: people refer to him either as "32", the number on his baseball shirt when he played for the town, or

The birds are a sign that there's a dead body nearby

as "Constable", his job title. While out on patrol one afternoon, he notices a lot of buzzards in the sky flying over one particular place. Since buzzards are a type of bird attracted by dead bodies, he decides to take a closer look.

The body is on the land belonging to the Rutherford family

He drives down a small dirt road, looking for a dead animal, such as a dog or a deer, that might be attracting the birds. When he doesn't find anything, he continues down to the creek, thinking he might find something there. He reaches a gate with a "No hunting" sign on it, which shows that the land belongs to the Rutherford Lumber Company. The Rutherfords are rich, and they own the mill in Chabot, as well as a large area of land covered in trees for their timber business.

He might have found the missing girl

The place Silas has stopped is very isolated. This is why he thinks the missing girl, Tina Rutherford, who "he was both hoping and hoping not to find under the cloud of buzzards" (P 10 / K 27) might be here. Tina, the daughter of the mill owner, is a nineteen-year-old student at "Ole Miss", the University of Mississippi. At the end of the summer, she left home to return to college, but never arrived there. Since then, every police officer in the state has been looking for her.

The town cannot afford a new police vehicle

Silas unlocks the gate and drives through. He hopes his Jeep will get stuck in the mud, because then he might get a new one. The one he drives is too old and not really suitable for the kind of roads he has to drive on, but the town does not have any money to replace it. He gets a message on his radio from Voncille, the town clerk. She wants to make sure he will be back in time to direct the traffic outside the timber mill during the shift change, and is annoyed to hear that she will have to do it herself.

"Plaid" is a pattern of different colored checks, often found on shirts

Silas gets out of the Jeep and slips and slides his way down to the creek. The closer he comes to the buzzards, the stronger the smell becomes. Finally he catches sight of the body: a few lumps dressed in plaid clothes, in the water surrounded by buzzards and flies. Although the birds have eaten a lot of the body and it has further decomposed in the heat, Silas knows who it is.

Later, Silas tells French, his boss, that he recognized the body because of the plaid clothes. A few days before, somebody had reported a burning car, and from the "M&M" on the vanity license plates, he had known that the car belonged to Morton Morrisette, who he had played baseball with at school. After giving up work due to injury, Morrisette had made money by selling marijuana. The police knew this, but had never arrested him because he was not selling hard drugs. On this occasion, the police had discovered that M&M had been seen with a well-known drug addict called Charles Deacon. A search of M&M's house had shown that somebody had been shot there and the body had been taken away. It was not until a few days later that they found M&M's hat in a tree several miles from his home.

M&M is too careful to get caught selling weed

Silas sits some distance from the body. The face looks horrific: swollen and partly eaten by the buzzards. His boss, Roy French, sneaks up behind him when he arrives, making him jump. He is pleased that Silas has not disturbed the crime scene, and he does not seem in any way affected by the terrible smell or sight of the body. Instead, he puts on some waterproof pants and goes down into the water to take photographs.

French does not mind the gruesome crime scene

French and Silas speculate about how the body came to be in this particular creek. They think that the killer must have been more intelligent than the drug addict Deacon, because M&M's hat was found somewhere completely different, probably put there in an attempt to confuse the police investigation. Next to arrive on the scene are two paramedics, or EMTs, and the coroner. One of them is Angie, Silas's girlfriend. The coroner does no more than confirm that the person is dead. The EMTs put on their protective clothing and go down to deal with the body. A local reporter and a couple more police officers arrive now, and Silas goes for a walk so that he does not have to watch the remains of the body being put into a bag.

EMT stands for "Emergency Medical Technician"

Later, in his office, Silas cannot stop thinking about M&M and wishing they had stayed in contact after high school. Really, though, he knows that that would never

Slias regrets losing touch with M&M

have worked out: M&M would not have been friends with a police constable. The town hall, where his office is located, is in fact just a one-room building, which he shares with Voncille, the only other full-time employee of the town of Chabot. Silas gets on well with Voncille, and she is sympathetic towards him after the death of his old friend. She asks Silas if the two of them had kept in touch. But they had not: the only people Silas really has any contact with nowadays are his colleagues, criminals and Angie.

Large chainstores in the nearby town have a negative effect on small local businesses

Being so small, Chabot only has a few buildings. Apart from the town hall, there is the mayor's real estate office, a post office, a bank, a combined diner and convenience store called The Hub, as well as a grocery store and a drugstore that will probably have to close down because there is a Wal-Mart in Fulsom, a nearby town. There is a bar called the Chabot Bus, which has been converted from an old yellow school bus, and where Silas and Angie often meet for drinks. Apart from this, there are just two more buildings, former offices that are no longer used, except by homeless people and drug addicts. Chabot was built on the edge of a gully that is covered in kudzu, a type of weed that is impossible to kill, and full of trash, which attracts wild cats and raccoons.

DUI is the crime of "driving under the influence", i.e. drunk driving

There is no ATM (automated teller machine) in Chabot, so its citizens have to drive 11 miles to Fulsom to get cash. Cell phones do not always work in the town. Chabot is located in Gerald County, which is "wet", i.e. alcohol is sold there. Since two of the neighboring counties are "dry" (the sale of alcohol is forbidden), a lot of people are caught drink-driving, and the DUI tally is high. Chabot is dominated by the lumber mill, which produces a lot of noise, dust and smoke during its three daily shifts.

Silas does not want anyone to think he and Larry were friends

Later, French comes into the office. He tells Silas that he had visited Larry Ott a few days before, because he is one of the "usual suspects" (P 23 / K 40) when it comes to missing girls. French notices that Silas calls him "Larry", implying that they were friends. Silas tries to deny any friendship: "I was in school with him's all." (P 23 / K 41) French says that he is planning to go back to Larry's shop later to try to frighten him into confessing. Silas is surprised to hear that, when French went to the shop earlier, it had been closed: "You ever know of him *not* being open during business hours?" (Ibid.) French thinks it does not matter whether the shop is open or not, as Larry never has any customers, but Silas knows that this is completely out of character for him. While French continues to joke around with Voncille, Silas remembers that Larry had tried to call him and had left him a message.

Without really thinking about it, Silas finds himself heading for Larry Ott's repair shop later that afternoon. Instinctively he feels that something is wrong. He thinks back to the couple of times Larry tried to contact him since his return to Chabot. The first time, Larry left a message on Silas's answering machine, asking him to call back, but he never did. A couple of weeks later, Larry called again, this time catching Silas at home. Silas is not comfortable talking to him, and ends the conversation as quickly as possible, saying that he is going out. Larry tells him he has just called to welcome him back. After the call, Silas almost seems to be in shock. He sits on his bed for a while:

Silas has resisted Larry's attempts to get back in touch with him

> "[…] remembering him and Larry when they were boys, what Silas had done, how he'd beaten Larry when Larry said what he'd said." (P 25 / K 43)

He knows that people have avoided Larry in recent years, but did not find out what really happened until he came back to live in the town.

Because he often drives past it, Silas knows it is true that Larry's business, Ottomotive Repair, has not had any customers since Larry took over from his father. Despite this, Larry goes there every day, hoping that somebody who does not live locally, and therefore does not know anything about him, might stop there in need of a repair. His business is in Fulsom, in a part of town that most other local businesses have moved away from. When he arrives, Silas sees that Larry's pickup truck is indeed

The people in the town do not want to have anything to do with Larry

missing. All of the equipment is old and has not been used for years.

Silas had driven past the shop from time to time and seen Larry standing there, watching the cars go by. However, Silas always avoided making eye-contact. Larry is ostracized by the local community because he took a girl to a drive-in movie when they were at high school and she was never seen again. Although her step-father wanted the police to arrest him, "no body was found and Larry never confessed" (P 28 / K 46). Silas had also known the missing girl, Cindy Walker: "In a way, Larry had introduced them." (Ibid.)

Many people believe that Larry killed a girl when he was at school

Silas still cannot imagine where Larry could be. He tries to persuade himself that Larry has finally taken a day off and is sitting at home, reading, but his instinct tells him that something is wrong. However, before he can investigate further, he gets a message from Voncille that somebody has found a rattlesnake in their mailbox and he needs to go and deal with it. Before he does so, he contacts Angie, asking her and her team to go and check out Larry's house. He calls it "following a hunch" (P 29 / K 47).

Silas is sure something is wrong

The place where the rattlesnake in the mailbox has been reported is in a part of town that Silas calls "White Trash Ave." (P 30 / K 47), a kind of trailer park where poor white people live. There are always lots of dogs running around, making it difficult for people like Silas and the mail woman, Olivia, to do their jobs safely. When he arrives, there are four women, a few boys and Olivia waiting for him. One young woman with tattoos introduces herself as Irina Mott and tells Silas that the snake is in her mailbox. The women joke around and, when Silas asks who might have put the snake there, they tell him they all have a long list of angry, jealous ex-husbands and ex-boyfriends who might be crazy enough to do it. A boy is sent to fetch a shovel, which Silas slides into the mailbox. The snake tries to attack, allowing Silas to push it back to the edge of the box then pull it out and throw it onto the ground. He then allows the snake to wrap its body around the handle of the shovel and uses

All of the women have dangerous ex-husbands and boyfriends

the spade to cut off its head. While all this is going on, Irina holds on tightly to his arm. Once the danger is over, Silas takes statements from the women, flirting with Irina as he does so. However, he then has to leave quickly to direct the traffic for the five-thirty shift change at the timber mill.

Irina is attracted to Silas

While directing the traffic and getting a lot of angry looks from the mill workers because the cars are not moving as fast as they would like, Silas reflects that this job was not exactly his dream:

He had other dreams when he was younger

> "[…] the drivers in cars on the highway glaring at him as if he'd chosen to be out here screwing up their day, as if this had been his life's goal, the reason he'd destroyed his arm pitching college baseball and joined the navy and then, discharged, gone to the police academy in Tupelo and spent ten years babysitting students at Ole Miss, breaking up frat parties, manning the gate at football games, giving DUIs, years of preparation to come ruin their day." (P 36 / K 54)

He had taken this job, a constable in a hamlet, thinking it would be different from the kind of police work he has been doing up until now. His cell phone rings and, although he is not supposed to answer it while on traffic duty, he does so. It is a call from Angie, who is now at Larry's house. Her only comment is "Oh my God" (P 37 / K 55).

Angie has discovered something bad at Larry's house

Chapter Three

INFO AT A GLANCE

A flashback to Larry's and Silas's first meeting

- Silas and his mother, Alice, are very poor.
- It is clear that Larry's parents and Alice have met before.
- Larry is a misfit at school: teased by the white kids and bullied by the black kids.
- Larry's attempts to be accepted by the white kids fail miserably.
- Larry and Silas become friendly when they are alone: Larry teaches Silas how to shoot.

Larry loves horror stories by authors like Stephen King

Larry is first introduced to Silas on a cold spring day in 1979. He and his father pass Silas and his mother at the side of the road one morning on their way into town. As usual, Larry is reading, but looks up when his father brakes. He immediately notices that the two strangers are not wearing coats, despite the freezing weather. His father drives on past them, but Larry gets him to stop, recognizing Silas as "a rabbit of a boy he'd seen at school, a new kid" (P 38 / K 56). He wonders why they are waiting at this particular place, a long way from anywhere.

Although he is clearly annoyed, Larry's father slams on the brakes and reverses back to the two people, opening the car door to let them in. Larry turns up the car heater to help them warm up. It seems that Larry's father knows them:

The woman is not a stranger to Larry's father

> "'Alice," said his father, pulling onto the road, 'introduce these younguns.'
> 'Larry," the woman said, as if she knew him, 'this is Silas. Silas, this is Larry.'" (P 39 / K 57)

The boys shake hands, Larry wishing he could give Silas one of his gloves, but unsure how to go about it. Because they smell of smoke, Larry realizes that they must live in an old log cabin for hunters on the edge of his father's land. It is a very basic place with no water or electricity, and just a wood-burning stove for heat. He wonders when they had moved in there, and who allowed them to do so. Meanwhile, Larry's father and Silas's mother talk about the cold. When he refers to Chicago, however, she is silent, and he turns up the radio in embarrassment.

Mentioning Chicago causes an uncomfortable silence

Larry pretends to read his book while observing the boy sitting next to him. He is "terrified of black kids" (P 40 / K 58), and now he goes to a school where most of the students, and many of the teachers, are black. His fear is fueled by the fact that the black kids are so different from him: he loves reading whereas they excel at sport:

> "Everything Larry couldn't do – spike a volleyball, throw a football or catch one, field a grounder, fire a dodgeball – these black boys could. Did. They manipulated balls as if by magic, basketballs swishing impossibly, baseballs swiped out of the air, fierce-eyed boys hurling and curving through their lives as smoothly as boomerangs." (P 40 / K 58)

Contrast between Larry and the black kids at his school

However, he notices that Silas, sitting next to him, is secretly reading his book, too.

Larry's father drops the boys off at their school. All of them are aware that it is "unusual" and "inappropriate" (P 41 / K 58) for black people to be getting out of a white person's car. Silas disappears as quickly as possible. As Larry passes Alice, he sees "how lovely she was" (ibid.). At lunchtime, Larry looks for Silas but does not see him. He cannot look too closely, because the black boys would beat him up if they noticed him. After school, he tells his mother what had happened. She is surprised and asks him for more details. However, when she asks where the two black people live, Larry pretends he does not know, because he "sensed he'd said too much already" (P 41 / K 59).

Blacks and whites do not mix

For the next three mornings, the woman and the boy are waiting for Larry and his father at the same place. Larry holds his book so that Silas can read it too while they drive to school. In the afternoons, Larry's mother wants to know all about the journey, especially whether his father and the woman had seemed friendly. One day, he tells his mother where he thinks they live. That evening, there is a strange atmosphere in their house. His mother announces that she will be driving Larry to school the next day. Larry feels bad because he has "betrayed a trust between himself and his father" (P 43 / K 60).

Larry's mother is clearly not happy about the two strangers

On the drive the next morning, Larry's mother slows down when she sees Alice and Silas waiting. It is clear that the two women know each other. Larry's mother gives each of them an old winter coat. When Alice makes no attempt to put hers on, Larry's mother speaks cruelly to her: "You've never minded [...] using other

They get warm coats but will have to make their own way into town from now on

people's things" (P 43 / K 61). She then drives away, leaving them at the side of the road.

Silas and Alice never get a ride from them again, and Larry now has to drive in silence with his father. He has always been aware that his father, Carl, likes "most everyone except him" (P 44 / K 61). As a young child, Larry was often ill, suffering from asthma and allergies and needing glasses. He is like the men on his mother's side of the family, who his father despises. He particularly disapproves of one of his wife's brothers, who not only is a vegetarian but also wears a seatbelt in the car, which Carl considers to be cowardly behavior. Larry even looks like his uncles, rather than having his father's "tall, pitcher's physique and blond curls and dark skin and green eyes" (P 45 / K 62).

Larry is not the strong, attractive son his father would have wished for

As well as being physically weak, Larry does not share his father's talent for mechanics. However, once he turns twelve, his mother persuades Carl to take him along to the shop, "Ottomotive". Larry works for his father, cleaning the tools and the shop floor, and finds that he likes the atmosphere of the place. When Carl's friends come round later in the day, though, Larry makes sure he stays away from them. These friends include their neighbor Cecil Walker and others who work at the mill. They sometimes come to get something fixed on their trucks, but usually they just want to have a drink, watch Carl work, and listen to his stories about various customers he has had, laughing at all his anecdotes. Carl clearly enjoys being the center of attention on these occasions.

To his surprise, Larry enjoys working at the car repair shop

Larry now keeps a lookout for Silas at school, and sees him talking and laughing with some of the other black boys. For Larry, Silas's behavior feels like a "betrayal" (P 50 / K 67), because he believes they have a special connection: "For hadn't Silas been his doppelgänger?" (Ibid.) So one Sunday afternoon, when both his parents are out, Larry borrows one of his father's guns and walks to the cabin. He normally goes in the opposite direction, towards the Walkers' house, in the hope of seeing the fifteen-year-old Cindy Walker sunbathing or smoking on

Larry feels a connection to Silas

He often watches Cindy Walker from a hiding place in the woods

their deck. Her step-father, Cecil Walker, often comes out to tell her off, and Larry fantasizes about her asking him for help.

Today, however, he heads in the other direction. He wonders whether it would be possible to make friends with Silas, given the society in which they live:

> "Having a black friend was an interesting idea, something he'd never considered. Since the redistricting he was around them constantly. The churches were still segregated if the schools weren't, and sometimes Larry wondered why grown-ups made the kids mingle when they themselves didn't." (P 51 / K 69)

White adults are hypocritical: they do not mix with black people, but their children have to do so

Larry does not fit in with either the white kids or the black ones at school. The white boys laugh at him and the black boys deliberately bump into him and trip him up. One day, Larry is on the swings with two white boys, Ken and David. Nearby there is a group of black girls, talking and laughing. Ken and David start imitating the girls and saying nasty things about them. They also talk about going to drive-in movies, to see the kind of horror movie that Larry longs to see, too. He dares to ask whether he could go with them sometime, and they tell him he can only come along if he joins their club. To do so, he has to go up to one of the black girls, Jackie Simmons, and call her "Monkey Lips" to her face.

None of the kids at Larry's school accept him

The bell rings for the end of break and everybody, including the teachers, starts to go back inside. David jumps off the swing and lands near the girls, making them scream and laugh. Ken does the same, also getting a reaction: "Them white boys crazy" (P 55 / K 72). By now, the girls, the teachers and the two boys are watching Larry to see what he will do. As he swings higher and higher, he knows how important his next move is for his future reputation:

David and Ken enjoy provoking the black girls

> "He thought if he could land in the center of them, scatter them, what a story it would make, he thought of going inside with Ken and David who'd tell everybody how far Larry Ott flew and how he sailed like a missile into the nigger girls." (Ibid.)

Larry sees a chance to change his status at school

He also knows that he could win some respect from his father if he was able to say he was going to a drive-in movie with his friends. Predictably, things do not turn out as planned. The girls are starting to walk away when he finally jumps, so Ken is the only one who sees him. He shouts "Monkey Lips" as he lands awkwardly and falls to the ground. A few moments later, he opens his eyes to see Jackie standing above him, challenging him to repeat what he said. She then walks off with her friends, who comfort her. Ken and David also hurry away, abandoning him. The girls tell one of the teachers and she comes over to him: "Ain't that girl got enough problems in this world without a white boy calling her that?" (P 56 / K 73) Larry is sorry, but the teacher says he has to apologize to Jackie. She also says that she should tell Larry's father what happened, but it would be a waste of time.

The teacher implies that Larry's father is a racist

Larry has to go back to his classroom, where most of the other kids are black. The teacher is also black, and the atmosphere is uncomfortable. After a while, the teacher asks the class to carry on reading and leaves the room. Immediately, someone throws a heavy textbook at Larry's head. One of Jackie's friends orders him to bring it back to her, aggressively referring to him as "white boy". All the other kids start laughing, including Ken and David, and suddenly most of the class start throwing their history books at him. He wants to shout insults at them, but cannot make himself say the words out loud. One of the girls starts pulling his hair. Larry still has a small hope that the white boys might help him, but they are laughing as hard as the others, "and he knew this was not going to happen any more than the drive-in movie would" (P 57 / K 75). It is only when the teacher comes back that Larry is released.

Larry cannot defend himself, and the other white kids do not help him

He knows the white kids will never really accept him

As Larry comes closer to the cabin, he sees that it must still be occupied. The cabin is very basic, with no running water or electricity. Just has Larry is considering trying to get closer to the cabin, somebody behind him says "Hey". Larry turns around, still holding the rifle, to see Silas with a big pile of firewood in his arms. When he sees the gun, Silas drops the wood and puts his hands

The cabin where Silas and his mother live is very run down, with no basic utilities

up: "You gone shoot me?" (P 59 / K 77) Larry reassures him that this was not his plan: "You scared me is all. Sneaking up like that." (Ibid.) He puts the gun down and holds out his hand to Silas. After a moment's hesitation, they shake hands. Silas asks what Larry is doing out there, and Larry tells him his father owns the land, and that he has been hunting. Silas asks to borrow the rifle so that he can shoot some squirrels for his mother to cook, guessing correctly that Larry's father must have several guns and would not miss it.

Larry teaches Silas how to use the gun. Silas shoots a few times, then, looking through the sight, turns slowly until the rifle is pointing straight at Larry. Larry is frozen with fear, but Silas does not shoot: "Now we even" (P 62 / K 80). He practices shooting again, saving the hulls of the cartridges. This makes Larry sad, realizing Silas does not have much of value. On impulse, he tells Silas to keep the gun for now. Realizing how late it is, Silas hurries to the hut with his firewood. Larry watches him go, but, before he leaves, he puts his gloves in a place where Silas will find them.

Silas frightens Larry in the same way that Larry frightened him

Chapter Four

INFO AT A GLANCE

Silas and French investigate Larry's house after the attack

- Larry has been found, badly hurt but still alive.
- Silas remembers the day he spent with Larry in his barn.
- It is hard to say whether Larry was attacked or tried to kill himself.

Back in the present, Angie reports on the phone to Silas about the condition they found Larry in: "Bad" (P 64 / K 82). He was lying in a pool of blood with one gunshot wound to the chest, holding the gun. It is too soon to say whether he will survive or not. Angie asks Silas if he's going to come to the hospital, but he wants to take a look at the crime scene. Silas nearly uses Larry's first name when talking about him: "I'm going on over to Lar– to Ott's" (ibid.), but stops himself just in time.

Silas wants to hide the fact that he and Larry were once friends

After speaking to Angie, Silas calls his boss, French, to tell him what has happened. French wants to know how the ambulance crew had known to go to Larry's place, and Silas hesitantly admits that he sent them there "on a hunch" (P 65 / K 83). French sends Silas to Larry's place.

The missing Walker girl used to live near Larry's place

Larry's house is near Amos, a community so small that Chabot seems like a big city in comparison. Even the local store has closed down, and now only a handful of mostly black people still live there. On his way, Silas drives past the home of the other missing girl, Cindy Walker. Nobody lives there now and the house is falling down. As he drives, he looks out for other tire tracks, but only sees those left by the ambulance and by a truck, probably Larry's.

This is only the second time Silas has been inside Larry's house

Once he gets to Larry's house, Silas can see a lot of footprints in the mud, but not much else. He looks at Larry's truck but does not disturb anything. He then goes into the small, wooden house that he still remembers from his one visit, many years before. He is careful not to step in the pool of blood on the floor, or to touch the pistol, which the ambulance crew had left behind.

There is nothing much to find in the house

Silas walks carefully through the house. The old gun cabinet is now stuffed full of books and mail. Larry's rooms is tidy, and also full of books: stories he had read when he was young, adventure stories, horror stories, and hundreds of book club catalogs. His childhood clothes are still hanging in the closet, along with his adult clothes. The bathroom is clean and bare, the cupboard containing little more than a tube of toothpaste. Silas looks through the rest of the house but does not find anything unusual.

Memories of a special day when Silas and Larry were kids

When he goes out of the back door, Silas sees more footprints in the mud. Carefully avoiding them, he walks over to the gate and stops when he reaches the barn. This brings back all the memories of his first visit:

> "He stood leaning on the gate and saw himself years ago, the day he'd come here. No grown-ups, no teachers, no other girls or boys, black or white, just him and Larry." (P 69 / K 87).

They had spent a fun day in the barn: climbing on the tractor, catching lizards and even a snake. Larry knows lots of complicated words, such as "herpetarium", meaning a reptile house. Inside the barn now, he looks around by the light of his flashlight. Beyond a door, he can hear noises and smell something strange: "For a moment he imagined it was a body" (P 70 / K 88). Taking out his pistol, he carefully opens the door. The sight of the hens fluttering around inside makes him jump and accidentally fire his gun. He laughs with relief.

The strange sounds and smells come from the hens

Silas is waiting on the porch when French arrives from the hospital. French tells him that Larry is still alive, but has lost "a shitload of blood" (P 71 / K 89). They look at the footprints, and identify the smaller ones as Angie's. They know that some of the others might give them a clue as to what happened, so make sure they eliminate their own from the investigation. Inside the house, French examines the gun. It is a .22 that has been fired once, and the serial number has almost been completely rubbed off. Larry himself is not allowed to own a firearm, so Silas wonders where this gun has come from: it might not even have belonged to Larry. French believes that Larry shot himself. Silas wonders whether Larry came home to find a drug addict in his house, who then attacked him. However, the fact that Larry's wallet had not been stolen and he had been shot at close range seems to speak against this theory.

The mystery of where the gun came from

Speculation: was Larry shot by a "crackhead"?

French looks around, expressing surprise that Larry does not have cable TV, or even a remote control for his old-fashioned television. He does not have an answering machine or a computer. French calls him a "frozen in the 1960s kind of character" (P 74 / K 91), and, as another example, talks about how old-fashioned his shop is. All of Larry's tools are hand-operated, whereas modern repair shops use power tools and computers. Silas points out that Larry does not need modern tools if he has no customers, and that maybe he prefers reading to watching television. However, they do find a brochure for DIRECTV, a company that installs satellite dishes. French notes that the house looks the same as it did when he was last there, one week ago (apart from the blood stain).

Larry has no modern appliances, neither in his home nor at work

However, French and Silas do find something unusual in the fridge: a case of beer with one can missing. Silas knows that Larry does not drink alcohol, and is not convinced by French's theory that Larry might have started drinking. French starts to do the forensic examination of the house, sending Silas outside to take molds of the footprints outside. They also check out the barn for signs of the missing girl.

Larry might have been attacked because of the missing girl

Before they leave, French says he will go to Oxford the next day to speak to some of the people who knew the Rutherford girl. Silas is instructed to return to Larry's house and see if he can find anything else. French thinks that the shooting might be connected in some way to the girl's disappearance. They secure the house with police tape before they go.

Larry has tried to contact Silas

Back home, Silas gets himself a beer. He thinks about calling Angie to say that he is too tired to meet up with her this evening. It is already eleven o'clock. Then he notices that the light on his answering machine is blinking. He presses 'play' and is startled to hear Larry's voice. Larry is asking Silas to call him back, even if it is late, because he has something important to say. Silas did not hear the message soon enough: "Well, it was late, wasn't it, Larry. Too late." (P 79 / K 96)

Chapter Five

INFO AT A GLANCE

The friendship between Larry and Silas comes to an end one summer

- The two boys have to keep their friendship secret.
- Larry takes Silas to spy on Cindy Walker.
- Silas defends Cindy against her step-father's abusive behavior: a black boy who dares to challenge the actions of a white man.
- Carl finds out that Larry has lent his rifle to Silas and orders him to get it back.
- He forces Silas and Larry to fight for the gun.
- Larry says something unforgivable to Silas.

The story returns to the year when Larry and Silas were friends. The summer vacation has just started and Larry is up early, looking forward to three months of freedom. His mother fries eggs for the family breakfast. Carl goes into the living room and switches on the television, as he does every morning. Soon he will leave for work: although he complains about working at the weekend, he actually prefers it to staying at home with Larry and his wife. Before he leaves, he tells Larry he has to stay outside and cut the grass: "Which meant *Don't read all day*." (P 82 / K 99) Their yard is large, three acres in size, so Larry knows it will take him at least half of the day to do the job. He decides to start right away and get it over with. As he starts work, he thinks about Alice and Silas, and how his father must have bought them their car. However, he knows now that he should not talk about this to anyone, that he should have kept his knowledge of the two people a secret. In a way, he had betrayed his father by telling his mother about them:

The start of the summer vacation

Carl thinks his son should be outside, doing a physical activity

> "He should have known that men do not discuss with their wives (or mothers) the business that is their own." (P 83 / K 100)

Now that Silas has got the .22 rifle, Larry carries a gun that looks similar, so that his father will not notice that the rifle is missing. Throughout the spring, he and Silas have been spending a lot of their free time together: shooting and playing other games that boys like to play, such as cowboys and Indians. Sometimes Larry caught snakes, although Silas always kept away from him then. When the weather got warmer, they fished together in the creek. Silas will not take any of the fish they catch home to cook and eat, because his mother does not want them to play together. "Is it cause I'm white?" (P 85 / K 102) Larry asks, but Silas says all he knows is that he had to promise to stay away from Larry. Larry is sure his color can be the only explanation for this. This is exactly why he would never tell his father about the friendship, but thinks that a black woman would be pleased if her child was friends with a white child:

The two boys have become friends

Silas had to promise his mother not to be friends with Larry

White people's attitude towards blacks

> "He'd assumed the anger that black folks felt was a reaction to white people's attitude toward them. *Yall started it.* But if somebody white was willing to befriend somebody black, offer them gifts, even a place to live, shouldn't the blacks be grateful?" (P 86 / K 102)

Larry has made a few attempts to get the rifle back, offering to swap the gun for a knife, but Silas is not keen. Larry knows he will have to get it back soon.

Silas's interests are changing

Today, Larry heads over to visit Silas after lunch. Because he knows his mother is watching him, he sets off in the direction of the Walkers' place so that she will not know where he is really going, doubling back once he is out of sight. Nowadays, Silas plays a lot of baseball at school, and Larry "worried that he was losing him" (P 87 / K 104). Silas has been to his house once, but Larry knows this will not happen again. He wonders if the time has come to share his "secret" about Cindy Walker. When he is near Silas's cabin, he stays just inside the woods and watches his friend practicing baseball. Larry starts reading his book, and soon Silas appears at his side, wanting to know what the stories are about. Then the two boys start walking, and, Larry telling Silas he has something, or somebody, to show him.

An example of the way Cecil treats his step-daughter: he can be dangerous

Silas does not see the funny side of the story

When asked, Larry admits that the person is a girl: "A real pretty one" (P 90 / K 106). He also tells Silas that the girl's step-father, Cecil, is crazy. As an example, Larry tells him a story about one New Year's Eve. Larry and Cindy are outside with Carl and Cecil, who are drunk. They are happily setting off fireworks, and everyone is laughing and joking around. But then her step-father thinks it would be funny to throw fireworks at her. One of them hits her, and she screams as it explodes. Then Cecil accidentally drops the lighted match he is holding, which sets light to the fireworks he has been keeping in his coat pockets. Everyone starts laughing as he runs around, trying to extinguish the fireworks. Larry laughs as he tells the story; Silas, however, does not: "Sound more mean than crazy [...]. I don't know if I want to go see a man like that." (P 91 / K 108)

However, the boys continue on their way until they reach the Walker place. Just before they get to the house, Larry lies down on his stomach, getting Silas to do the same. They are hidden by the woods and have a good view of the porch from where they are. Instead of Cindy sunbathing, they see Cecil and Carl, smoking and drinking beer. Larry wants to go, but Silas wants to stay: "We snuck this far. Maybe that girl'll come out." (P 92 / K 109)

So Larry and Silas stay hidden, watching the two men. After a while, Cindy appears on the porch, wearing just a small towel. Watching, Silas whispers that he has seen Cindy around at school. The argument on the deck becomes more heated; then Cecil reaches over and pulls on Cindy's towel. Cindy tries to slap his hand away, but he keeps tugging until she is half-naked. At first, Larry's father looks too, but then seems embarrassed.

Cecil starts to get physical with his step-daughter

Before Larry realizes what is happening, Silas jumps up and strides across to the deck. The two drunk men are too astonished to speak as he confronts them: "Yall leave that girl alone." (P 93 / K 110) Cecil lets Cindy go and Cindy, who is astonished as the men, stares for a moment before going back into the house. The action brings Cecil to his senses, and he demands to know who Silas is, but Silas is already walking, then running, away. Larry slowly retreats to the bottom of the hill and is just about to get up and leave when his father appears at the top. Carl looks around, and Larry is glad he is still hiding in the leaves. Then Cecil calls Carl away.

The black boy dares to confront the white men

Larry finds Silas practicing baseball again. He thanks Silas for helping Cindy, but Silas accuses him of spying on people. Larry avoids the question of whether he has ever been on a date with Cindy. Silas then goes back to Larry's first comment:

Strong contrast between the reactions of the two boys

> "'You wasn't gone help her.'
> 'I wanted to.'" (P 94 / K 111)

Silas heads for home, and Larry follows him. Silas runs ahead and throws the baseball back to Larry, who tries to catch it but misses. Silas is angry that his ball has disappeared into the bushes.

Carl has discovered that his rifle is missing

As soon as Larry gets home, he is in trouble. His father calls him into the kitchen and demands to know where his rifle is. Larry admits he has lent it to a friend. His father responds sarcastically: "I didn't know you had none." (P 95 / K 112) Under further pressure, Larry finally confesses that he has lent it to Silas. Carl's reaction is frightening:

> "His father moved his face so close Larry could smell beer and cigarettes, and in that moment he knew that Carl had seen him at the bottom of the hill. 'Just a dad-blame minute. You gave my gun to your nigger friend?'" (P 95f / K 112)

Larry's mother is very upset that the two people are still living on their land

Carl shows his dislike for his wife and son

Larry's mother, hovering in the background, tries to intervene, telling her husband to stop. Carl turns his sarcasm on her, asking if they should invite Silas and his mother round for dinner. He then orders Larry to get the rifle back the next day. Larry's mother demands to know how long Silas and Alice are going to be living in the cabin: "It ain't proper." (P 96 / K 113) She gives her husband an ultimatum: "If they don't leave [...] then me and Larry are. Tonight." (Ibid.) It seems for a moment that Carl is going to start laughing, but instead all he says is "Don't tempt me" (ibid.). His wife almost seems to be pleading with him, but he turns his attention back to Larry. Larry is to get the gun back the next day, no matter what. Carl then storms out of the house.

Larry's mother is very protective of him

As she always does, Larry's mother comes into his room that evening when he is in bed. Today he ignores her. When he was younger, she prayed that his asthma attacks and stutter would go away. She also always prayed that Larry would find a special friend, "one just for him" (P 97 / K 114). Her prayers have been answered, even though it has taken a long time. Both his stuttering and his asthma have disappeared, and he has found a friend in Silas. The only problem is that he cannot tell her about that.

Larry tries to soften Silas up with a present, but he still does not want to return the rifle

The next morning, Larry leaves the house without his mother seeing him and heads over to Silas's place. He stays out of sight until Alice goes to work and Silas comes out. Larry greets his friend, then gives him a book of short stories as a peace offering. Then comes the difficult part of his visit: once again, he tells Silas that he must give the gun back. Silas argues that Larry has got a lot of guns and he only has the one. Larry starts to plead with him, but before they can get much further Silas notices something. Larry knows straight away what it is: his father is coming towards them, drunk and aggressive. He has been following Larry and abuses him because he did not realize his father was behind him:

> "You ain't got the slightest idea what's around you, you and your monster books. In the olden days you'd a been dead long time ago. Some Indian cutting your throat or some gook with a grenade. You got it easy. Momma's boy reading the livelong day. […] But you can't unscrew a god dang bolt to save your life, can't change a dad blame battery. And here when it comes to knuckles, you can't even get your own daddy's gun back from the boy that stole it." (P 100 / K 116f)

Carl shows what he really thinks of his son

Carl then turns his attention to Silas, who refuses to look at him. Silas claims he has not stolen anything. Carl says that, if this is the case, he does not need to be offended. He begins to play the two boys off against each other: "Peers like we got us a dispute between the races here" (P 101 / K 117). He demands to know who Silas's father is, and is told that he is dead. This results in more sarcasm: "Dead! Well, ain't that sad. And he didn't leave you no gun?" (Ibid.) He comes up with an idea to solve the dispute. He tells Silas and Larry that they have to fight for the gun.

"Peers" means "It appears that / it seems that"

At first Silas refuses, but Carl threatens him. He goads them on, saying that it will be an even fight since Larry, although older, is "on the girly side" (P 102 / 118). Silas still resists, but then Carl says he will whip them with his belt if they refuse. This is what finally makes Silas push Larry a couple of times, but not very hard. After the third push, Larry grabs Silas, but Silas frees himself easily by kneeing Larry, making him drop to the ground, out of breath. Carl orders him to get up again, hitting him with the belt when he does not do so immediately. Larry feels a deep sense of shame at the whole incident, but does finally start wrestling with his friend. His father urges them to fight dirty. Silas pushes Larry's face down into the ground and they know the fight is over. Larry

Silas easily wins the fight: Larry appears weak and helpless begs Silas to let go, starting to stutter in his need to breathe properly. "Looks like you won yourself a rifle, boy" (P 103 / K 119) is Carl's response. However, Silas pushes down harder, and Carl mocks his son's stutter. It is only when Larry manages to gasp out the insult "you n-n-n-nigger" (ibid.) that Silas finally lets go.

Larry struggles to his feet and looks at Silas, seeing that he is really angry now. Silas hits him hard and he falls to the ground again, with blood in his mouth. He is very sorry for what he said to Silas, knowing that everything has changed between them now. Carl is so drunk that he is swaying, nearly falling over, and leans on Silas to steady himself. Silas struggles to free himself and runs into the woods, almost in tears. Larry and his father are left alone.

Chapter Six

INFO AT A GLANCE

Silas makes a surprising discovery while looking through Larry's house

- Silas looks for more clues at Larry's shop and in his house.
- He finds a photograph of his mother.
- There is a flashback to Silas and his mother's trip south from Chicago.
- The journey was difficult: most of their possessions were stolen on the way.
- They end up moving into Larry's father's old hunting cabin.
- Silas secretly keeps the photo.

Larry is still alive

The morning after the attack on Larry, Silas sits at The Hub, having breakfast. He has already called the hospital and found out that Larry has not recovered consciousness. Silas is relieved, as this means he does not have to go and see Larry yet. All this time he has used Larry's insult "as an excuse to avoid him" (P 105 / K 121). When he was at university, he did not come home very often, and he never asked about Larry while he was there. Sometimes when he was hanging out with some of the other guys, like M&M, they would start talking about him, even suggest going over to his place to rough him up. However, Silas never wanted to talk about his old friend or have anything to do with him.

Marla, the cook at The Hub, is very motherly towards Silas, making sure he has enough to eat and even giving him some extra hot dogs for later. She has heard about what happened to Larry and asks how he is doing. She shows some sympathy for Larry. Although nearly everyone else thinks he is a criminal, she remembers him as a polite, extremely shy boy: "Wouldn't hardly look you in the eye." (P 107 / K 123) However, she has not seen him for a few years now, ever since one of the girls that worked on the register in The Hub told Larry he was not welcome there anymore. The girl had been fired, but Larry had not come back.

Marla is one of the few people who does not see Larry as a murderer

Once again, Silas goes to look around Ottomotive. There are practically no other businesses in this part of town, and Silas wonders whether the others have moved away so that they did not have to be near Larry's shop. He unlocks the office door and looks around, but does not find anything unusual. There are, however, books everywhere, not surprising considering Larry's love of reading. Apart from the books, all he finds are tools. Silas thinks back to the time when his mother died and he drove back down south for her funeral. He has to pass Larry's shop on the way and sees Larry standing at the door of his business, looking out. Silas, however, ignores him:

> "Silas had kept his eyes forward, as if Larry could've seen him, as if he'd been standing there all those years, watching for Silas to come back." (P 109 / K 125)

Larry makes Silas feel uncomfortable now: he wants to avoid any contact

Silas feels very uncomfortable about this, and deals with his mother's affairs as quickly as possible after the funeral so that he can leave again. As he passes Ottomotive on his way back to Oxford, once again Larry is standing in the same place. And once again, Silas pretends not to see him.

Next, Silas returns to Larry's house. Now, in the daylight, he notices some small pieces of broken glass on the ground, from a car windshield or a window. There are only a few pieces, as if somebody had cleaned up the rest. Silas picks them up as evidence. He continues walking slowly round the yard to see what else he can find. In

There is evidence that someone else has been at Larry's house recently the field beyond the barn, he spots some distinctive tire tracks and makes a mold of them. While waiting for the mold to dry, he sits on the porch and notices something else in the grass: "Roach end of a joint, dewy, dirty, probably useless, but still." (P 110 / K 126) Silas is absolutely sure that Larry had never smoked weed, and that someone else must have dropped the roach.

Larry never really had anyone to talk to or share things with before he was friends with Silas

In the barn, he realizes the chickens are hungry and feeds them. Being in the barn brings back more memories for him. He thinks about how he used to go fishing with Larry, and how much he had learned from him:

> "[…] the boy always talking, full of information about snakes or catfish or owlets or lawn mowers and dying for somebody to tell it to." (P 112 / K 128)

Silas returns to the house and starts to look through everything carefully. There are, of course, lots of books, many of which he remembers from when Larry used to tell him the stories. After a while, he notices the trap door leading to the attic and fetches a chair so he can climb up there. The attic is dusty and full of boxes. Silas looks through the documents he finds. Larry's father had once owned a large amount of land, but by now Larry has sold nearly half of it to the Rutherford Lumber Company, the only way he has of earning money. In another corner of the attic, he finds a filing cabinet full of folders containing search warrants issued by French, receipts for Mrs. Ott's nursing home bills, gas bills, phone bills and other household paperwork. He also finds a shoe box of old photos, and takes that downstairs with him, along with the phone bills.

Silas searches for clues in Larry's paperwork

Back in the kitchen, Silas looks through the phone bills. The only calls listed are local ones. However, he also finds bills for a cell phone: all of the calls received have come from one number. At times the calls were fairly regular; at other times infrequent. Silas makes a note of the number. The shoe box contains a random selection of photos, mostly of Larry as a child and teenager. One photo shows Larry as a baby, sitting on a black woman's lap. Silas is shocked when he recognizes the woman as his own mother.

He discovers something unexpected

When Silas was thirteen, the comfortable life he had been living in Chicago changed forever. He and his mother had been living with her boyfriend, Oliver, when he was arrested for assault. They were living in a quiet, black neighborhood, where the people were relatively well off. He has only seen the projects, where a lot of very poor blacks live, on television. He has not, however, met many white people at this point in his life, and does not do so until he and his mother move south.

"The projects" are an area with very high crime rates and other social problems associated with poverty

Alice's boyfriend, Oliver, is not around very much because of his job as a delivery man. When he is there, he ignores Silas, and would prefer it if the boy did not exist. On this occasion, Oliver's attempt to escape from the police has failed, and they have caught and handcuffed him. After a search, the police find the weapon they are looking for and arrest Oliver. As he is being taken away, he tells Alice to get a lawyer for him. She raises enough money for bail, but when he is released, he tells her that there is another warrant out for his arrest, and once the police realize and come to arrest him again, he will have to go to prison for a long time. Alice is ordered to hold a yard sale of their possessions and get what money she can. Ignoring Silas, he says goodbye to Alice and is out of their lives forever. Alice manages to make some money from the yard sale, and, by the time the police come back, looking for Oliver, she and Silas have also left.

Alice's boyfriend does not want Silas around

As they leave Chicago on a Greyhound bus, Silas asks his mother where they are going. All she will say is that they are going south: "Cause I got people down there." (P 117 / K 132) Silas wonders if one of those people might be his father, but Alice tells him to be quiet and read his magazine. At this moment in time, Silas is not sorry that they are leaving Chicago, although, when he is older, he realizes that it was not a bad time in his life:

Alice does not really want to talk about where they are going and why

> "He always had hot food and his own room. TV. Laughing his head off at J.J. on *Good Times* […]." (P 117 / K 133)

He'd gone to a good school, had lots of friends and learned to play baseball there. Now he is heading into the unknown. He looks at each new place they stop at with fascination. When he and Alice get off the bus, in

They have to sell some of their possessions to make it easier to continue their journey

Memphis, he is farther from home that he has ever been before. His mother had an address for a place to stay, but, after dragging their heavy suitcases there, they discover that the building is no longer in use. So they turn around and head back to the bus station, but along the way, it becomes clear they have too much luggage. Spotting a pawn shop, they go inside and the owner goes through the contents of their suitcases. Alice has had some of these possessions for most of her life, yet she is offered very little money for them.

Alice is clearly uneasy and is trying to work out what to do

Silas and his mother continue their journey, arriving in Jackson, Mississippi, later that evening. They only have two suitcases left now, and the white driver helps to carry them off the bus. The town seems very small and quiet to Silas compared to Chicago, with very few people around. The bus driver asks them where they are going, and Alice replies that they want to find a motel for the night. The driver tells them that there are no motels nearby, only "nicer" hotels. Alice thinks she knows what he means by this: "You mean won't take black folks?" (P 119 / K 135) The driver, however, assures her that he simply means the hotels are very expensive. He offers to drive them to a motel in his truck, as he has just finished his shift. Alice does not want him to go to any trouble, but he insists. He asks Alice and Silas to wait for him. While he is gone, Silas asks whether they are really going to go with him. His mother looks around. The streets are deserted and there are no restaurants where they could go for a few hours. Silas cannot wait in silence, but keeps nagging his mother about what they are going to do. Finally, when he refuses to be quiet, she slaps him, the first time she has ever done so in public. Instinctively, he turns to run away, but she catches hold of his wrist:

They do not want to go somewhere with a white man but have few other options

> "'Don't you dare run,' she said, 'from the one person in this world who love you.'" (P 120 / K 136)

Silas knows his mother is upset, but cannot help making things harder for her

Silas accuses her of not knowing where they are going. Although he can see that she is close to tears, he cannot stop himself from complaining: "I'm cold, Momma. I want to go back." (Ibid.)

The driver returns and introduces himself as Charles. Alice tells him their names and makes sure Silas shakes his hand politely. His mother gets into the front of the truck with Charles, but Silas insists on sitting in the open back, refusing to share the driver's cabin. He knows he is embarrassing his mother and avoids looking at her. He hears her try to excuse his behavior with a joke. From the back of the truck, Silas can see Charles talking to his mother, who is sitting as far away from him as possible. Silas shivers with cold and thinks about jumping out of the truck when it slows down. Although he is still young, he understands the situation that is unfolding here:

> "Silas knew what the bus driver wanted with his mother, and he thought how he, Silas, was in a way an impediment. Without him here, she could do whatever she needed to, without witness, to get through this cold night, to get wherever she was going. He knew his mother was beautiful." (P 121 / K 137)

He realizes his mother may have to sleep with Charles to get a warm place to stay

Silas is still trying to decide whether to jump off the back of the truck. He gradually realizes that they are not being taken to a motel. Charles is telling Alice a story and Silas knows his mother will laugh at it, "because it was polite and she lived in a world where she had to be polite all the time" (P 122 / K 138).

Charles is not taking them to a hotel after all

Silas does not want to be part of this world. He wants to get away from his mother, so picks up his backpack and jumps off the truck, determined to find a train to take him back north. He runs down the street and hides behind a garbage can in an alley. Charles's truck drives past slowly and he can hear both Charles and his mother calling his name. He nearly responds to the panic in Alice's voice, but instead puts his fingers in his ears so that he cannot hear her, then runs again. After a while, however, it is his turn to panic. He has lost all sense of time and space. Suddenly, somebody pulls him behind a couple of garbage cans and takes his backpack, coat and shoes. His muggers search through his pockets, stealing the few cents they find there, along with his pocket knife. One of the thieves puts his hand over Silas's mouth, but Silas bites him and starts to shout for help.

Silas tries to escape

Charles saves him from his attackers

Charles appears and pulls the thief, a black boy around Silas's age, away while the other one runs off. The boy curses Charles and pulls away from him so hard that his sleeve tears off. He runs away, too.

The reason Alice and Silas had no coats when Larry and his father first pick them up: they had been stolen

Alice hugs Silas, relieved to have found him again. Silas himself realizes that the worst is over now. When the three of them get back to the truck, Charles curses when he discovers his hubcaps have been stolen. Silas and Alice's other suitcases have also gone, along with Alice's coat. Amazingly, she has still got her money. They all get back into the truck, and Alice apologizes to Charles for all the trouble they have caused him. He tells them that they are unlikely to find a room at a respectable motel at this time of night, but Alice is prepared to go to anywhere now. Charles offers to drive them. Cold and exhausted, Silas falls asleep, and when he wakes up, Alice seems happier and more relaxed in Charles's company. He goes back to sleep and when his mother wakes him, he sees that they are at a bus station, and it is already six o'clock in the morning. He is told to stand outside the door while his mother talks to Charles. While he is waiting, shivering with cold, the door to the bus station opens behind him. The woman who has just unlocked the door is astonished to see Silas standing there and tells him to come inside "before you freeze to death" (P 124 / K 140). The woman, whose name is Clara, asks Silas if he is alone. She corrects the way he speaks to her, insisting that he calls her "ma'am". She correctly guesses that he is from the north:

Here in the south, black people are expected to take a respectful tone when they talk to whites

> "I can tell. You don't talk like the colored boys around here." (P 125 / K 140)

Alice turns up a few minutes later. By this time, Silas is drinking hot chocolate that Clara gave him. She has also found a pair of sneakers in the lost and found that he can have. Silas wants to say something to Alice, but she tells him not to talk to her. They go to a diner and Alice orders a big breakfast for Silas. She herself says she only wants a coffee. She does not watch Silas eat, but stares out of the window. The waitress brings her more coffee, and Alice asks if they may sit in the diner for a while longer, until it is time to get their bus. The waitress says that they can. Silas finds it hard to believe that his mother is not hungry. Finally, her patience with him seems to snap:

> "'What's missing out of you, Silas?' She looked hard. 'You ain't seen it that bad. I know. I know cause I have seen it that bad. But you. Up till now you had it easier than I ever did. But now I see what kind of man it's made of you, I don't know if maybe I didn't do you a disservice.'" (P 126 / K 141f)

Alice is irritated by Silas: he does not understand what she is going through, because he has had an easy life up until now

Finally, she tells him her plan. They are now in Fulsom, Mississippi, and are going to take the bus to Chabot. They are going to stay at a place she knows, and life will be quite basic at first. She promises that things will be better once she gets a job, but if Silas is going to come with her, he will have to change his attitude.

She needs her son's support for their new life

The waitress returns to their table with a second plate of hot food. When Alice protests, the waitress tells them somebody had sent it back to the kitchen, and if they do not eat it, it will be thrown away. Alice asks Silas to go and sit at another table so that she can eat alone. He does not really understand why, but does so, watching her from a distance. He looks around the restaurant but does not see anyone who might have sent a meal back. After his mother has paid the bill, Silas sees her leave a generous tip, and then ask the waitress for a job application.

The waitress shows them great kindness and gives Alice a free meal

Silas and his mother catch the bus to Chabot, from where they get a lift to Amos. They buy a few things at the store there, then walk along a dirt road to the cabin. Alice asks him to get some firewood. It is the first time she has spoken to him since they were in the diner.

Now, twenty-five years later, in Larry's kitchen, Silas is lost in his memories. He has not seen his mother's face for many years, because most of their possessions had been stolen on their journey south. The picture is not perfect:

It means a lot to Silas to see a photo of his mother after so many years

> "The smile she wore was the one she used around white people, not the one he remembered when she was genuinely happy, where every part of her face moved and not just her lips, how her eyes wrinkled, her hairline went back, how you

> saw every gleaming white tooth, the kind of smile he'd seen fewer and fewer times the older she got. But this plastic smile, the photograph, was better than no picture at all." (P 128 / K 144)

Silas decides to take the photo with him, although he knows he should not remove anything from a crime scene. He feels guilty, but tells himself that nobody will miss one photo.

Chapter Seven

INFO AT A GLANCE

The story of what happened on the evening Cindy Walker disappeared

- Larry is going to take Cindy on a date.
- His mother is very excited about his first date, and even his father is supportive.
- Cindy is the one who asked Larry to take her out.
- Her step-father is violent towards Larry and contemptuous of Cindy.
- Cindy reveals the real reason why she asked Larry out.
- When she does not turn up again, Larry is suspected of having harmed her.
- Larry's family is destroyed by the accusations.

It will be the first time Larry has been out with a girl

The story continues in a flashback. It is now 1982 and sixteen-year-old Larry finally feels like a different person, because he is going to take Cindy Walker out on a date. His mother, clearly excited, tells his father about it. His father is astonished: "I'll be damn." (P 130 / K 145) His mother presses him for details about how he asked her, but Larry is embarrassed to talk about it.

Larry would never have dared to ask Cindy out: the date is her idea

The truth is that Larry did not ask Cindy out. Instead, Cindy had come out to talk to him when he had been passing her house. He feels awkward even talking to her. She asks if he likes movies, and whether he has ever been to the drive-in theater. He knows it is a place where boys go with their dates, somewhere they can drink beer, smoke marijuana and kiss in private. Cindy suggests that she and Larry go there, and asks if he can get a car. Naturally, Larry would do anything for her: "If he had to steal one he could." (P 130 / K 146)

When Larry lets slip that they are going to the drive-in, he is embarrassed by his father's reaction: Carl thinks it is funny, since the drive-in is well-known for showing R-rated movies. Larry pretends they are going to see a western, but his father does not believe him. He tells Larry to take the Buick as there is more room on the back seat, and even offers to pay for the outing, passing his son a twenty-dollar bill:

Carl is not shocked by the idea of Larry making out with a girl: in fact, he encourages him

> "He could have slid a thousand-dollar bill and Larry wouldn't have been more surprised. For a moment he couldn't imagine what to say." (P 132 / K 147).

Carl still drives Larry to school every day, in silence. They have never spoken about what happened on the day that Larry and Silas fought. Later that evening, Carl had returned home as if nothing had happened, and gradually, over the next few days, life had returned to normal.

As far as Carl is concerned, the fight between Larry and Silas might never have happened

Now that Larry is older, he goes to a different school, one where the numbers of black and white children are more evenly balanced, which makes life easier for him. Today, he cannot help boasting to Ken and David about his upcoming date. They cannot believe he is dating any girl, let alone Cindy Walker: "She wouldn't go out with *you*." (P 133 / K 149) At break, he goes to find Cindy, knowing that she will be smoking with her friends under the bleachers near the baseball field. He sees Silas and his friend M&M practicing. When Cindy sees him waving to her, she leaves her friends and goes to talk to him. He tells her about the movie, but Cindy does not seem very interested. Larry agrees to pick her up at seven, and to bring some beer. Seeing Silas watching him, he waves, hoping that he has been seen talking to Cindy, but Silas turns away.

Larry wants the other boys to know about his date

Larry seems very immature in comparison to Cindy

Time drags for Larry that week as he waits for Friday evening to come. His mother keeps asking him about Cindy, whether he has spoken to her, if she is excited about their date. Larry, however, is reluctant to talk about it. He knows that Cindy does not seem very excited about the idea of going out with him, and seems embarrassed to be seen with him. Ina reminisces about her

Larry is naive enough to think there will be a second date

first date, when the boy took her fishing. Larry is already thinking ahead to the possibility of a second date.

Larry is worried about what will happen if he goes to join the other white boys, but does not dare refuse

On Thursday lunchtime, Larry sits near the other white boys and watches Cindy from a distance. Ken calls him to come and sit with him and his gang. Larry is nervous about this invitation, but obeys. David asks him if he has got a condom, and when another boy, Philip, asks why, reveals that Larry has got a date with Cindy Walker. The reaction of the other boys is: "She's a slut" (P 136 / K 152). Uncomfortable, Larry reacts to Philip without thinking:

> "'I heard she likes niggers,' Philip said.
> 'Yo momma likes niggers,' Larry said quietly. Before he'd thought.
> For a moment their table became the incredulous calm eye of the cafeteria's hurricane, the boys looking from Larry to Philip […]." (Ibid.)

He gets away with insulting one of the cool boys

For a moment, nobody knows how this is going to end for Larry, but then Ken laughs and everything is all right. Even Philip does not take offense, and, when Ken asks about the movie they are going to see, all of the boys join in the conversation. Larry is so happy that he cannot even eat, thinking about how he has "a date the next day and friends to tell about it" (P 137 / K 152). After lunch, David gives him a condom. Larry puts it in this wallet next to the twenty dollars from his father.

Larry's mother has started to irritate him by talking so much about his date

Before he can leave for his date, Larry has to keep his promise to get Cindy some beer. He cannot let his father see him take it from the refrigerator. His mother is still excited for him and keeps giving him advice about how to behave towards Cindy. He nods and manages to take a can of beer without her seeing, which he then hides in his room. He returns to the kitchen for another one. When his mother asks him about the movie yet again, he manages to answer without losing patience with her. From in front of the TV, Carl calls to Larry to bring him a beer. He warns his son not to let Cecil Walker have any of his money, and says he wants his change after the date. Larry takes one more beer, knowing that Carl might notice if there are too many missing.

During the evening meal, which Larry can hardly eat, his parents talk about the places they used to hang out with their friends when they were dating. There was a special tree with a rope attached, which the boys used to swing off. The tree was very tall, and the rope swung out over a gully, so there was an element of danger. Carl tells a story about a time when he and his friends persuaded Cecil Walker to take a swing on the rope, although he was afraid of heights and had been drinking heavily. For three dollars, Cecil agrees. Since he comes from a very poor family, all he is wearing are cut-off jeans. Cecil climbs the tree, but falls instead of jumping off at the right moment. The other boys hear him scream as he falls into the gully, and think for a moment that he might even be dead. However, shortly afterwards, they hear him swearing, and somehow he manages to climb back up out of the gully, scratched and bleeding. The other boys cannot stop laughing at the sight of him, and after a moment he starts laughing too, and demands his money because he has won the bet. Larry asks where the tree is, but it has been cut down and taken to the mill.

Larry's parents talk about their youth

Cecil's family were as poor as black people

Carl seems to remember Cecil affectionately

The time has finally come to pick Cindy up, so Larry drives to her house. Seeing Cecil on the porch, Larry casually goes over to him, still smiling as he thinks about the story he has just heard, and greets him by his first name. Cecil, however, is clearly not in the mood to be friendly:

Cecil is waiting to confront Larry: he demands respect in a way he has never done before

> "'Boy, it ain't Cecil today ner ever again. It's Mr. Walker now, got it?'" (P 143 / K 158)

He insists that Larry addresses him as "sir", and orders him to come closer. Larry still thinks that Cecil might be having a joke with him, when the older man grabs him and pushes his face into the wall. He comes close enough for Larry to be able to smell his breath. He threatens Larry with physical violence "If you so much as get a finger in her" (P 143 / K 159), and squeezes his testicles to make his point, calling Larry a "sissy boy" (ibid.). Larry collapses in pain, unable to speak and feeling as if he is going to be sick. It is Cindy who saves him by appearing on the porch and pushing Cecil away. Her step-fa-

Larry is helpless in the face of Cecil's attack

ther calls her a whore. She goes inside to speak to Cecil for a moment, then comes back and the two of them walk to the car.

Right from the start, the date does not go as Larry had imagined

Cindy asks Larry to move over onto the passenger seat, where she is sitting. At first Larry thinks she wants to start kissing him right there and then, but she slips out of the car and gets into the driver's seat. She is not happy that he has only brought two beers along with him, and that they are warm. She starts the car, flipping her middle finger to Cecil as they screech off down the dirt road. Larry is nervous about Cindy driving and is afraid Cecil will tell his father. He asks her if she even has a driver's license.

Cindy is using Larry

As they drive away, Cindy reveals the real purpose of the evening. She wants Larry to do her a favor and drive her to Fulsom to see her boyfriend. She had asked Larry to take her out as he is the only person Cecil will allow her to go out with, reckoning that nothing will happen between them. Larry does not really know how to react to this turn of events, but Cindy appeals to his good nature:

> "'You have to help me. Nobody else will. That Cecil's after me, and if I can't go see my boyfriend, I'll never get away from him.'" (P 146 / K 162)

She wants Larry to pretend to be with her all evening so that she can see her boyfriend

Larry still has not completely understood the implications of what is happening, and asks why they cannot simply go on their date. Cindy then confides in him that she is pregnant, but refuses to say who the father is: "If Cecil finds that out, he'll kill him, too." (P 147 / K 162) She wants Larry to drive around for a while, then go to the drive-in at the start of the second movie, when there will be nobody taking money. He can park near the back, and nobody will see that he is alone. Her boyfriend will drop her off on the road to her house and Larry is to pick her up there at eleven o'clock and drive her home, as if they have been together the whole time.

Larry has no choice but to do what Cindy wants

All the dreams Larry has had about this evening have been shattered. He knows now that he will never get to kiss Cindy at the back of the drive-in. He makes one more attempt to change her mind, but she refuses. Once again, she emphasizes that he is the only person who can help her. When she reaches her destination, a dirt road some way beyond Fulsom, she makes him swear to be at the meeting place at eleven. As he drives away, he sees her running to meet her boyfriend. He does what she has asked him: he drives around, then goes to the second movie and parks at the back. When he has been there for a little while, he recognizes Ken's father's car. The driver seems to be looking for him, and parks directly behind him. Larry realizes that the people in the car will be able to see that he is alone, so he takes a blanket and puts it over his hand, holding it up to make it look like somebody's head. In the rearview mirror, he sees that it is Ken and David in the car, and Ken is now getting out and coming towards him, trying to see what is going on in the Buick. Larry starts the car and drives off quickly, still holding up his other arm to maintain the illusion of the girl.

Ken and David have come to spy on him

Larry pretends Cindy is with him in the car

Larry arrives early at the agreed meeting point, hoping to spot Cindy's boyfriend. He speculates that she might be seeing an older man. However, eleven-fifteen comes around and there is no sign of her. At eleven-thirty, Larry starts to think that her boyfriend must have dropped her off early, although then surely Cindy would have waited for him, since she wanted to pretend she was with him. He looks for her along the road, becoming more and more worried. As midnight approaches, he gets out of the car and looks around, wondering if Cindy and her boyfriend have had an accident. He cannot imagine how he would explain this scenario to Cecil and his father. However, he has not quite given up hope that he has somehow missed her, and slowly drives around again, hoping Cindy will appear and start yelling at him. But there is "no mad girl in his lights" (P 151 / K 167), just the trees.

Cindy does not turn up at the agreed time

By now, Larry realizes that his own parents will be wondering where he is. He wonders if Cindy has been drinking and has passed out somewhere by the side of the road. He turns off the car lights, afraid of attracting Cecil's attention. Larry keeps trying to reassure himself that everything will be all right, that there will be some

Larry tries to persuade himself that he is worrying for no reason kind of explanation for her failure to appear. But by this time he knows that he has to go right up to the house and find out whether Cindy is there.

Cecil violently attacks Larry, demanding to know what has happened to Cindy

Turning the corner to the Walker house, Larry sees that everything is dark. This puzzles him, because he thought there would be a light on for when Cindy's mother gets home from work. He is about to reverse away from the house, when Cecil suddenly appears, furious and demanding to know where Larry has been. Cecil drags him out of the car window and pushes him up against the car: "Where is she?" (P 152 / K 168) Larry says that he thought Cindy was already home and claims he dropped her off, managing to escape from Cecil's grasp. However, Cecil knocks him to the ground, wanting to know where Larry let her out of the car. Larry cannot speak because Cecil is almost strangling him. He is only saved by Cindy's mother returning from work.

Larry feels ill at ease inside Cindy's home

A little while later, Larry finds himself inside the Walkers' house for the first time, waiting for the police and for his own parents to arrive. Cecil's wife, Miss Shelia, cleans up and makes coffee, insisting that Cecil stops drinking beer now: "You don't want to be drunk when the law gets here." (P 153 / K 169) When the sheriff arrives, Larry, of course, has to stick to his story about dropping Cindy off in the woods. He tells the sheriff they went to the drive-in and left during the second movie. He keeps his promise not to reveal that Cindy is pregnant. The sheriff does not seem too worried about the affair:

At this point, the sheriff does not believe anything has happened to Cindy

> "Teenagers, he said. Wasn't no point in getting all worked up. She was probably out with some boy and would show up later that night." (Ibid.)

After Cindy's mother admits that this is the kind of thing she might do, the sheriff seems reassured. He tells everyone to go home and call him in the morning if Cindy has not turned up by then. Cecil is the only one who is still upset. Just before he leaves, the sheriff stops Larry and pulls his lockblade knife out of his back pocket. Although Larry says that all boys have a knife like this, the sheriff takes it away with him.

However, when Cindy does not turn up in the next few days, things start to get difficult for Larry. Ken and David tell the police how they had apparently seen the two of them speeding out of the drive-in. This makes it seem that Larry has not been telling the whole truth, and he is called in to the sheriff's department with his father "for the first of many 'talks'" (P 154 / K 170). Larry now admits that Cindy had told him she was pregnant, but he had not revealed this straight away because he had promised not to. In the sheriff's car, almost as if he has been arrested, Larry is driven to the place in the woods where he claimed to have dropped Cindy off. He is asked to look around for tire tracks, cigarette butts or anything that might prove his story about a waiting car. There is nothing to find. The tone becomes more accusing:

The sheriff's attitude towards Larry begins to change

> "Well, the sheriff said, hadn't Larry worried about leaving a young girl alone in the woods? What kind of a gentleman would do that?" (Ibid.)

Larry is made to feel that he has behaved badly, that everything is his fault

When asked, Cindy's friends claim they have no idea where she might have gone and say that she did not have a boyfriend. The police begin to search the Otts' land for Cindy's body, and interview Larry again and again. Larry never goes back to school, but spends his time at home, reading. His father starts to drink heavily, whiskey instead of beer. The Ottomotive car repair shop loses most of its customers, until people from out of town passing through are the only ones who stop there. Carl is usually drunk, and has become a man "who'd stop talking to his son period and quit telling stories" (P 155 / K 171). Larry's mother no longer goes to church, and often seems distracted at home, not really knowing what she is doing. Things will never be the same again for any of them, not unless the truth about what happened ever comes out:

Cindy's disappearance gradually destroys the Ott family

> "Their lives had stopped, frozen, as if in a picture, and the days were nothing more than empty spaces on a calendar. In the evening the three of them would find themselves at the table over a quiet meal no one tasted, or before the television as if painted there, the baseball game the only light in the room, its commentators' voices and the cracks of bats and cheers the only sound, that and the clink of Carl's ice." (Ibid.)

Larry and his parents are not really living anymore, just existing

Eventually, about a year after Cindy's disappearance, Larry leaves home to join the army. He is allowed to go because, although by now nearly everyone believes he raped and murdered Cindy, no evidence of any kind has been found. His commander in the army has been told about his situation and has agreed to send Larry back to Chabot to stand trial if necessary. Larry discovers that "the anonymity of army life" (P 156 / K 172) suits him. He becomes fit, loses weight and is kept busy all day. While in the army, he is trained to be a mechanic, discovering that he does have a talent for it after all. He is friendly towards the other soldiers but does not socialize with them, preferring to spend his time alone. Whenever he goes home, his parents are "both older and stranger" (P 157 / K 172). His mother is clearly starting to suffer from dementia. His father cannot look him in the face anymore; he spends as much time out of the house as possible, and the rest of his time slumped in front of the television. One evening, Carl crashes his truck while driving drunk and dies of his injuries.

Larry gets on well in the army because nobody bothers him there

After three years in the army, Larry is honorably discharged and sent home to look after his mother. Silas no longer lives in Chabot, and there has still been no trace at all of Cindy. The Walkers have moved away and their house has fallen into disrepair. At some point, Larry takes his mother to live at River Acres, a nursing home. Every morning he listens to the sound of trees being cut down on the land he has sold to the mill. Larry spends his days waiting for customers, his evenings reading and his nights alone, remembering how his mother had prayed for a special friend for him, and what had happened when that prayer had been answered.

"Honorable discharge" means leaving the army having done your duty well

Chapter Eight

INFO AT A GLANCE

Silas discovers an unexpected connection between himself and Larry

- Silas tells Angie a lot about his personal life, and almost reveals a secret.
- He goes to see Larry in hospital, but Larry is still unconscious.
- He visits Larry's mother and tries to tell her what has happened, but, because she has Alzheimer's, she cannot understand him.
- Silas realizes the truth about who his father was.
- He comes across Wallace Stringfellow, illegally driving a four-wheeler.

The story returns to the present day. Silas arrives at the diner where his mother used to work, opposite the courthouse. He does not come here very often, but being here today makes him feel close to his mother, "dead so long with her secrets. And his" (P 159 / K 174). The waitress recognizes him and tells him she read about him in the paper, in an article about the M&M case.

Silas's mother had worked in the diner for 20 years

Angie arrives and Silas thinks about how good she looks. She realizes something is wrong, and he tells her he has been thinking about Larry, and has been asked to work on the case of his shooting while French tries to find out what has happened to the Rutherford girl. The general opinion is still that Larry shot himself, but Silas remains unconvinced: "Why now, though? […] After all this time, why shoot his self now?" (P 161 / K 176) Angie thinks it might be because Larry killed the missing girl, but Silas still does not believe that. Angie disagrees: Larry may have been kidnapping girls for years but had never been caught. Or perhaps he had suppressed the urge to kill, had not been able to stop himself from attacking Tina Rutherford, and had then panicked when he realized who she was. Silas argues that maybe Larry did not kill "that first girl" (ibid.), i.e. Cindy, but even here Angie believes the events of that time might have affected his behavior:

Silas disagrees with his boss about what happened to Larry

Unlike Silas, Angie believes Larry might be guilty

> "Maybe everyone thinking he did's finally added up for him. All those years of nobody talking to him. You think he ever gets laid? Man with his rep? Maybe he finally snapped and said to himself, 'All right, if they gone treat me this way then where's the nearest girl?'" (Ibid.)

Silas opens up to Angie about his past

When she asks Silas why he does not believe this, he admits that he had been friends with Larry at school. He tells Angie about how he and his mother came to live in the south, how he had met Larry and his father, how Ina, Larry's mother, had given them warm coats and how his mother had come home with a car one day but never told him where it came from. He tells her how he came to like living in this part of the country once he got used to how different it was from Chicago, and how getting the rifle and playing baseball had given him a sense of belonging. He goes on to tell her about the fight, and how after that he and his mother had moved into a house trailer in Fulsom that Alice had saved up for. By this time he was well-known locally as a baseball player who often had his name in the paper. Larry, on the other hand, was "just a hick that nobody liked" (P 163 / K 178).

He explains how he gradually felt at home in this part of the world

Larry had never really had any friends but had wanted attention from the other kids

Angie asks for more details, and Silas tells her that Larry was strange, different from the other kids. He lived too far away to have any friends and did not have the kind of social life other kids his age had, preferring to read. He would bring things to school, such as snakes he had caught, "trying to make people notice him" (ibid.). Silas suddenly remembers a time when Larry had come to school with a monster mask at Halloween:

> "It was a zombie mask with fake hair and rotting skin made of heavy plastic and red with gore, as realistic as anything anybody had ever seen, like a real severed head." (P 163f / K 178)

Larry's zombie mask is the same mask that his attacker was wearing

Larry gets a lot of admiring attention because of the mask, even from the cheerleaders, several of whom try it on. Another group of girls asks him to come to their church's Haunted House that evening and wear it in one of the rooms. Of course, Larry agrees. When Silas gets to the party, Larry is already there, wearing a sheet as part of his costume, but Silas ignores him when he waves. Larry spends the next three hours in one of the rooms in the haunted house, giving the party-goers a thrill. Silas watches from afar, "thinking that tonight Larry must've felt almost normal" (P 164 / K 179).

At the end of the party, Larry comes out of the house and wants to join the others:

For once, Larry feels he has been accepted

> "He stood, waiting to be noticed, congratulated on his performance, maybe, welcomed by the group, given a beer." (Ibid.)

Silas mentions that Cindy Walker was part of the group, and is annoyed at himself for letting the name slip out. He tells Angie how he and the others had just ignored Larry. Larry had hung around for a long time, still hoping to be included in the party. But nobody reacts to him, and in the end he has no choice but to drive home. When he has left, Silas, Cindy and the other burst out laughing. Silas can see from Angie's face what she thinks about this behavior. She asks him how long before Cindy disappeared all of this happened, and he tells her it was a couple of months. Angie then wants to know whether Silas had ever dated Cindy, but he does not answer her question. He avoids the question by saying Cindy's step-father was the kind of person that black boys stayed away from if they had any sense. Angie then expresses surprise that Cindy had gone out with Larry if he was "such a loser" (ibid.), but she is called back to work before Silas can say any more. However, Angie promises that they will continue the conversation later, especially since this is the first time Silas has ever told her about his past.

Nothing has actually changed for Larry: the other kids still want nothing to do with him

Silas goes to the hospital to check up on Larry. The volunteer at the reception desk, Jon, recognizes Silas from the newspaper. He checks his computer and tells Silas that Larry is still in intensive care. Before he goes up, Silas asks if Larry has had any other visitors. Jon does not think he has, but promises to ask the other volunteers, and to let Silas know if anyone comes to see him from now on. Upstairs in the intensive care unit, Silas discovers from the nurse that it is "amazing he's still alive" (P 168 / K 183), and that it is still uncertain whether he will recover or not. Larry is lying in a bed, attached to machines, pale and lifeless. Silas will have to speak to the doctor to find out more about his prognosis. Since nobody has told Larry's mother what happened yet, Silas feels it is his duty to do so. He drives out to River Acres

Silas finally goes to see Larry in the hospital

Larry could still die of his injuries

Larry was clearly unable to afford a good nursing home for his mother

nursing home and, seeing it up close for the first time, realizes how run down it is. He recognizes the black man in uniform just inside the front door as someone who he had once arrested for drunk driving. When he asks where he can find Mrs. Ott, the man simply nods in the right direction without even looking at him. He comes to an empty desk behind a sliding glass window and rings the buzzer. The woman who appears also recognizes him: she went to the same school and used to watch him play baseball. She seems surprised when he tells her he has come to see Mrs. Ott, explaining that her Alzheimer's makes communication difficult:

Mrs. Ott's health is very poor now

> "Most times she ain't know anybody. Can't move her whole left half. Just be laying there." (P 170 / K 185)

The nurse tells him that, when Mrs. Ott has an occasional good day, she calls her son and asks him to come and visit her. She had done so the previous day, but Larry had not turned up. Silas tells her that Larry has been shot.

Larry's mother does not recognize Silas, and Silas barely recognizes her, either

Ina Ott is in a double room with an old black woman in the other bed. The nurse, Brenda, tells her that Silas has come to talk to her about her son, but Mrs. Ott seems alarmed by his presence. For Silas, Mrs. Ott is also almost unrecognizable now. She has lost a lot of weight, and seems suspicious of him. She confuses him with Clyde, the man working at the front door. Silas tries to explain who he is and that he was friends with her son. However, Mrs. Ott is clearly having a bad day today, and does not even seem to know who Larry is. She asks how her chickens are doing, which are named after the wives of American presidents. Silas reassures her that he is taking care of the chickens, but her only response, again, is "Who are you?" (P 172 / K 187). After a while, Silas gives up, asking Brenda to call him if Mrs. Ott happens to have a good day.

Silas cannot make her understand who he is or why he has come

Outside the nursing home, Silas cannot help thinking about the day he spent at Larry's house, all those years ago. One incident from the day stands out in his mind: he discovered a lawn mower and asks Larry whether he gets to cut the grass. For Larry, this is a chore rather than a treat: "Get to? [...] You mean have to." (P 173 / K 187) But Silas has never mown grass before, so Larry shows him how to work the mower and lets him do it. Silas loves the sensations involved in cutting the grass. Larry sits on the porch and watches him for a while, then suddenly jumps up and pushes Silas away from the mower. Silas protests, but Larry says there is not much time left. Silas does not care, and carries on mowing, the job nearly finished by now. Then he sees headlights approaching, and knows that Larry's father is on his way home. Abandoning the mower, he runs to the fence and jumps over it, escaping into the woods just in time. Larry starts pushing the mower, as if he has been doing the work all along. When his father sees the yard, he praises him: "Good work, boy" (P 174 / K 189).

Cutting grass with a mower is a new experience for Silas

The one time Carl praises Larry, it is for work that Silas has done

Silas, who has crept back to watch them, overhears this. He also sees his friend's reaction:

> "Larry turned and pulled the mower toward the barn, looking over to where Silas had run, staring, it seemed, directly at him." (Ibid.)

Silas has never forgotten about this, as it was the time when he "had felt, most acutely in his life, the absence of a father" (ibid.). As he walks home, across the five hundred acres of land owned by Larry's father, he starts to become very angry. His mother is already home, with food from the diner and chocolate milk for their supper. She asks where he has been, but he tells her he got lost in the woods.

Back in the present, remembering that day, Silas comes to realize the truth about his background:

> "So he'd had a father all along, and not some deadbeat black man who'd knocked up Alice Jones and left, but a white man who'd slept with his maid and then sent her off to Chicago when she got with child." (P 175 / K 190)

Silas is Larry's half-brother

As he drives along, he decides to go and see whether the cabin is still there. On the way, he comes across a young man riding a four-wheeler, quite fast, down the middle of the road. When the man sees the police jeep, he throws a can of something into the weeds at the side of

A four-wheeler is an off-road vehicle, like a motorbike with four wheels instead of two

the road. Silas pulls him over. The man sits up straight when he spots the police uniform, and greets Silas in a friendly tone. Silas tells him he is not allowed to drive the four-wheeler on the road and asks to see his driver's license. The man's name is Wallace Stringfellow.

Silas wonders whether Wallace is a member of the Ku Klux Klan

When asked, he denies he has been drinking, although he admits to throwing the can away. Silas notices a pillowcase stuffed behind the seat and wonders "would it have eye holes, though in truth today's racism seemed less organized than when he'd been a boy" (P 176 / K 191). He tells Wallace that he is on Rutherford land and is trespassing if he drives there. Because he still wants to see the cabin, he lets Wallace off with a warning, but says he will get a ticket the next time he catches him on the highway. The boy does not seem very upset by this threat: "Yes, sir. Preciate the warning" (P 177 / K 191), and drives off.

Wallace's attitude towards Silas is rather cocky

Silas's mother had sacrificed everything for him, yet he had pretended she did not care

Silas drives back to Larry's place and leaves his Jeep there. He takes off his shirt in an attempt to cool down, and walks across the overgrown field towards his old home. As he gets closer to the cabin, he cannot stop thinking about his mother. To be able to buy them the trailer home, she had had two different jobs as well as working as a cleaner on the side. He had pretended to himself that his mother had sent him away to college in Oxford because she did not want him around. She had sent him money every week so that he would not have to work, but could concentrate on his classes and on playing baseball, yet still he had lied to himself about her motives. It is only now that he admits the truth to himself:

> "He knew now that she'd loved him despite his never writing her back, despite the trouble and fear he caused her, despite the thing missing out of him." (P 177f / K 192)

Alice had missed her son terribly while he was away

Back then, Silas had seldom come home to visit his mother. On these visits, she had always spoilt him, could never do enough for him, yet this had embarrassed him more than anything else. He always spent the evening with old school friends rather than with her, refusing to see "that she was starving from loneliness" (P 178 / K 192).

Today, Silas sees how overgrown and uncared-for the land has become. The place is so overgrown that he almost bumps into the wall of the cabin without seeing it. He has to push back vegetation to find the front door, which has an old padlock on it. He goes round to a window and shines his torch inside, seeing their old furniture still standing there. The window is locked from the inside, so Silas makes his way around the rest of the building, until he comes to a window which he can see has been opened. Somebody has broken the glass and unlocked the window. He does not touch it, but shines his torch through it. Someone has been in there and, when he directs the light to his old bed, he can see that someone has dug a grave underneath it.

The cabin is completely overgrown with vegetation

It seems that Silas has found the place where the missing girl is buried

Chapter Nine

INFO AT A GLANCE

Larry makes a new friend, Wallace Stringfellow

- Larry discovers that a young boy has been breaking into his barn and scares him away by wearing the zombie mask.
- Ten years later, the boy, Wallace Stringfellow, starts to visit him.
- It turns out that Wallace has been fascinated by Larry for many years.
- Larry considers Wallace the first friend he has had since Silas.
- Wallace has an unhealthy obsession with Cindy's disappearance.
- Larry misses Wallace when he stops visiting.

Larry is now thirty-one, his mother has just moved to a nursing home and he lives alone in the house. Around this time, he notices that somebody has been going into the barn while he is not home. His mother still knows who he is then, asking him about the shop and wanting to know how her hens are doing. He mentions that somebody keeps going into the barn and she tells him to lock the door, since it is an attractive place for children looking for adventure. Larry knows from personal experience that this is true, "remembering the boy he'd been there, the boy he'd been then" (P 181 / K 195).

Larry understands why the barn is tempting for kids

The one positive aspect of his mother's Alzheimer's is that she has completely forgotten about Cindy Walker's disappearance and everything that followed. Unlike Lar-

For Mrs. Ott, the incident with Cindy never happened

ry, she does not see any connection between the events of that time and the break-ins in the barn. Larry thinks of a way to put a stop to it. One day, he stays home from work and hides in the barn, up the hayloft. When he hears someone walking towards the barn, he puts on his old zombie mask, climbs down from the hayloft and hides near the back door. A blond boy, dirty, tanned and without shoes, comes in. Larry steps out from his hiding place "with his arms raised and his fingers claws and yelled, 'Argh!'" (P 182 / K 196). The boy jumps out of his skin and runs away as fast as he can.

Larry uses the zombie mask to frighten off the intruder

Larry's mother is pleased when he tells her what he has done: "That should fix him" (ibid.). She tries to tell the old black woman in the next bed, but the woman's dementia prevents her from responding. Over the years, it is only people like this, unaware of their surroundings and with no family to complain, who are made to share a room with Ina Ott, the mother of a possible murderer. Gradually, Mrs. Ott loses her memory, too, until all that is left is a thin woman, "waiting, without knowing it, to die" (P 183 / K 197).

Some families would protest if their relative had to share a room with Larry Ott's mother

Ten years after the incident, the boy Larry frightened in the barn returns. Larry is sitting on his porch, reading and drinking a coke as he does every evening after work. Hearing a vehicle approaching, he looks up. However, although he is the only person who lives around here, he cannot imagine that anyone is coming to see him. The driver must be lost, or it is someone coming to do some kind of damage to his home. He stands up and waits to see what will happen.

The van that pulls up has DIRECTV painted on the side. To Larry's surprise, the driver seems to have come to see him. He takes something from the passenger seat, then gets out and walks up to Larry, introducing himself as Wallace Stringfellow. Larry greets him politely: "What can I do for you?" (P 185 / K 198) He can smell alcohol on Wallace's breath as he shakes his dirty hand. Wallace tries to sell Larry a satellite dish, but Larry says he does not need one.

Wallace Stringfellow reappears in Larry's life

Even though Larry does not want to buy anything from him, Wallace seems reluctant to leave:

> "What if I just set a spell, then?' Wallace asked. 'Been a long one. I ain't gone bite.'
> 'Yeah,' Larry said. 'I'm sorry. I just don't get that many visitors.'" (P 186 / K 199)

Wallace creates a break in Larry's evening routine

Larry suggests they sit out on the porch. He sees from the clock that it is nearly time for the news, but he goes back out to join his visitor instead. He offers Wallace a drink, but has to tell him that there is no alcohol in the house. Wallace asks his name, and, hesitantly, Larry tells him. However, the name 'Larry Ott' does not seem to mean anything to Wallace. He asks Larry where he went to high school. They discover that they both went to the same one, and both left before graduating: "Couple a dropouts ain't we." (P 187 / K 201) Wallace sees that Larry was reading, and asks him what the book is. He has seen the movie version, and again tries to persuade Larry to get satellite TV: "You get you a dish? You ain't got to worry about reading." (Ibid.)

The two men have some things in common

Then Wallace turns to more personal matters: "Say your name's Larry Ott? Ain't I heard of you?" (Ibid.) Larry admits that most local people know who he is. With a grin, Wallace says he knows Larry is supposed to have killed a girl back in high school. He does not seem upset about this: "You famous. [...] Or *in*famous." (P 188 / K 201) Larry thinks that Wallace will not want to sell him a satellite dish now that he knows who he is dealing with, but Wallace assures him he does not care. He promises to come back on Monday, collects his things and drives away. Later that evening, Larry thinks about him. He knows that Wallace was lying to him, but does not mind. He also realizes Wallace is the boy he frightened off in the barn.

Wallace seems more excited than disturbed by Larry's reputation

On Monday evening, instead of reading, Larry simply sits on his porch, waiting. He is "disappointed but not surprised" (P 189 / K 203) when Wallace does not turn up. In fact, two months pass before he comes back, when Larry no longer expects to ever see him again. This time, he arrives on his four-wheeler, with some cans of beer in

Larry hopes Wallace will return, but he does not do so for several weeks

a brown paper bag. He offers one to Larry, who refuses. After a while, Wallace surprises Larry by saying "You don't like me much, do you" (P 190 / K 204). The boy watches the older man very intensely, waiting for his reaction:

There are parallels between Larry and Wallace

> "It's okay [...]. Not many folks do. All thank I'm weird. Why I quit school, got tired of em making fun of me." (ibid.)

Larry says that it is not a case of not liking Wallace; he does not know him. He admits that he does not get many visitors. Wallace makes a joke about it, and Larry cannot help smiling, something he very seldom does when someone else is around. He tells Wallace that his only other visitors in recent months have been a group of drunk teenagers who drove up to the house and threw beer bottles at it, calling him names and demanding that he come out. One of them smashed the headlights and windshield of the truck with a baseball bat before driving off. What he does not tell Wallace is that he had not been all that upset about the vandalism, as repairing the lights and windshield had given him a job to do the next day. Wallace's reaction is that he would have shot at the teenagers, but Larry does not have a gun. Wallace then asks why he does not have a dog, but Larry is allergic to them. Wallace tells Larry about his own dog, and the dogs he'd had previously, all of which had been killed in various accidents. The way he talks about these animals makes him seem callous: he does not seem to care if they died unpleasant deaths.

Teenagers drive to Larry's house to intimidate him

Wallace thinks Larry needs a dog or a gun to protect himself

Larry decides to change the subject by asking Wallace if he had really ever worked for DIRECTV, and Wallace admits that he had not. The van had belonged to his mother's boyfriend, who does work for the company. He borrowed the van as a way to make contact with Larry, to find out what he is like first-hand. Once again, he asks Larry for a drink, but when Larry tells him he still only has Coke, Wallace leaves, because "[o]nce I start dranking, I don't like to stop" (P 195 / K 209). Larry turns down both the offer of a satellite dish and a loan of Wallace's dog.

Wallace is a heavy drinker, whereas Larry does not drink at all

The next time Wallace comes to visit, he asks Larry if he has ever been married, or whether he has a girlfriend. The answer to both these questions is 'no'. He starts to get rather personal, asking if Larry is "one of them forty-year-old virgins" (ibid.). He talks about various women that he has sex with, and offers to drive Larry over to one of them who will have sex with him for money. Larry responds with his usual politeness: "Preciate it, no." (P 196 / K 209) This time, Wallace has got a whole case of beer with him, and Larry is worried about how drunk he is getting. On this evening, Larry tells Wallace he knows that he was the boy who had been in the barn, and Wallace admits it. He then reveals that, although he was too scared to go back into the barn after that day, he had often returned and fished in the creek nearby.

Wallace wants to know about Larry's sex life

Although he never went back to the barn, Wallace often returned to the Ott land

Wallace tells Larry how he had come to hear about him. He had heard gossip from other kids at school:

> "All the kids talking about it, that creepy fellow that went there same as us, that sat in some of them very desks we was in, how you abducted that girl and done away with her." (P 197 / K 211)

The teachers had responded to the talk about Larry by telling the children to forget about him, to stay away from him because he might be dangerous. Wallace, however, has deliberately done the opposite by coming to bother Larry, although Larry says Wallace is not bothering him.

Wallace seems to have become fascinated with Larry and his crime

Wallace then reveals that he has seen Larry before, at a church in a nearby town, about eleven years previously. On this particular day, Wallace had been outside the church with a few other kids, who had started talking about "Scary Larry" and wondering if he would come back again. One of their mothers had then told them to come back inside, and Wallace had taken a seat near the back, to keep a lookout. And then, after the service had started, Larry slipped in and sat at the back, too. Other members of the congregation noticed him and whispered. Just before the end of the service, Larry quietly left. Wallace followed him, even called after him, but Larry did not turn around. Larry realizes that he remem-

Wallace's first sighting of Larry

bers the incident, remembers how he had "called 'Hey' in a way he'd not heard before, not angry but curious" (P 199 / K 213). He had noticed Wallace in the church and the way he had kept looking at him: "Because of that boy, more than anything else, he hadn't returned." (Ibid.)

Wallace's scrutiny of Larry in the church had made him nervous

Wallace has been drinking beer all evening, but complains that it is not giving him a buzz. However, he has something with him "that'll get my head right" (ibid.), and proceeds to roll himself a joint. Larry is uncomfortable about this development, as he does not want to get into trouble with the police. Wallace is scornful of this, saying that there are no cops anywhere nearby. Larry watches him with interest, never having seen a joint before, but refuses to take a toke. Wallace tells him he gets his marijuana from a guy called M&M, who Larry remembers. They sit companionably together on the porch, Wallace smoking and Larry watching the sunset.

Wallace tries to get Larry to share a joint with him

On Christmas Eve, Larry is at home, thinking about his plans for the next day. He is going to visit his mother at the nursing home and take her some Christmas presents. It is several weeks since he last saw Wallace. At around midnight, he is woken up by the sound of somebody outside on the porch. Looking out of the window, he cannot see anybody, and so he opens the door quietly. There is still no sign of anyone, but just as he is about to go back inside, he spots something on the rocking chair. It is a shoe box, tied with a ribbon. Larry takes the box inside and opens it cautiously. It contains an old .22 pistol, still in good working order. It has recently been cleaned, and there are also cartridges in the box. There is a message: "Merry Xmas, Larry, from Santa" (P 202 / K 215).

A mysterious midnight visitor on Christmas Eve

The gun Larry was shot with was given to him as a present

On New Year's Eve, Wallace reappears, bringing fireworks with him, which they shoot across the open field. Larry tells Wallace about getting the pistol and hints that he knows it was from Wallace. The younger man pretends to know nothing about it. Setting off the fireworks reminds Larry of the New Year's Eve with the Walker family, all those years ago. Wallace is the second

It was Wallace who left the pistol

person he tells the story to; unlike Silas, Wallace thinks it is funny. Once again, they spend the evening together, Wallace drinking beer and Larry rocking in his chair.

After that evening, Wallace starts to come round once or twice a week. One day, he asks Larry about Cindy, whether he really killed her. He would like Larry to admit it, but Larry says that he only took Cindy on a date; nothing else happened. Wallace wants to know whether they had sex, and why not. He asks Larry if he is gay, but Larry says no. Wallace is pleased, saying that he hates gay people.

Wallace wants to talk about what happened to Cindy

Another time, Wallace reveals that he used to play in the old hunting cabin when he was younger. He had enjoyed the thrill of being inside Scary Larry's cabin, while wondering if this was where Larry might have hidden the girl's body. He goes on to tell Larry about a fantasy he had back then:

Wallace had tried to find Cindy's body

> "I used to imagine you'd find me playing in there and tie me up and keep me prisoner. But instead of killing me you'd just keep me out there and we'd get to be friends." (P 204 / K 218)

He tells Larry that he would not mind if he had killed Cindy, that they would still be friends. He hardly seems interested in Larry's denials. His attitude is that women sometimes deserve to be raped, even killed, but that he would never turn a friend in to the police, no matter what that person had done. He seems strangely obsessed with the case: "So if you did kill her, I'd like to know's all. How you done it. If you raped her." (P 205 / K 219) He says that some women like being raped, and has clearly fantasized about doing so himself. Larry, uncomfortable, tries to make him stop talking about it, and when he does not, says it is time for him to go to bed. Inside the house, he locks the door. He calls out to Wallace that he should go home and come back another time when he has not been drinking. Wallace seems upset, then suddenly becomes aggressive:

Wallace is aroused by the idea of raping a woman

> "He banged his head on the window again and kicked the wall. 'You fucking freak,' he yelled, 'I'm gone go tell the law on you right now, how you said you done it, killed that girl, told me ever thing –'" (P 206 / K 220)

Wallace turns on Larry, but still cannot get him to confess

This finally gets a reaction from Larry. He goes back outside to confront Wallace: "I ain't never hurt nobody in my life" (ibid.). Again, he tells Wallace to go home. Still shouting, Wallace goes over to Larry's truck and smashes the headlights and windshield. He carries on raging until he is tired and finally drives away. Larry stands inside his house, watching him from the window.

Larry tries to contact Wallace when he does not come back

The next day, Larry replaces his broken windshield for the second time. There is no sign of Wallace. When a month has passed without him turning up, Larry starts to worry, even looking up his phone number. There are nine different Stringfellows in the phone book. When he tries the first number, the woman who answers knows who is calling before he has even said his name. He hangs up, and a man calls back a few moments later, threatening Larry if he ever calls again. Larry realizes that people have caller ID nowadays, and gives up the idea of trying to reach Wallace by phone.

Larry clearly misses Wallace and hopes he will come back

However, he still hopes that Wallace will return one day. A couple of months later, in May, he buys a case of beer at the supermarket in case he ever does. He tries a few sips one evening, but pours the rest away. Sometimes he takes the pistol and aims it at birds, but does not shoot. In June, he actually has two customers in his shop, and starts to think he might need an assistant. He decides to offer Wallace the job, if he ever sees him again, to teach him a trade and give him a purpose in life, a reason to stop drinking and smoking pot. Larry even imagines passing the shop on to Wallace when he dies.

He remembers the church his mother used to go to after Cindy disappeared, a sect that, among other things, asked its members to fast for three days at different times of the year. Although Larry had never gone to the church with her, he had joined her in fasting, being "hungry for God" (P 209 / K 223) himself. The beginning of the fast was the hardest to bear; the pain of not eating became easier to bear until it no longer hurt. He did not know how hungry he actually was until he ate again:

> "Wallace's visits had shown him that being lonesome was its own fast, that after going unnourished for so long, even the foulest bite could remind your body how much it needed to eat. That you could be starving and not even know it." (Ibid.)

Until Wallace came along, Larry had had no idea how lonely he was

He now includes Wallace in his nightly prayers, hoping that God will help him.

Chapter Ten

INFO AT A GLANCE

Silas finally admits the truth about his relationship with Cindy

- Silas has found Tina Rutherford's body.
- Larry, still unconscious in hospital, is suspected of her murder.
- Silas volunteers to guard his hospital room at night.
- Convinced that Larry is innocent, he wants to stop him from confessing.
- Silas opens up to Angie about his relationship with Cindy.
- He has been carrying the guilt about Cindy's disappearance around with him for twenty-five years.
- Larry comes out of his coma.

Silas is exhausted. He has not been getting much sleep, and is struggling to keep awake on traffic duty. A week has passed since he found Tina Rutherford's body in the old hunting cabin, and he has now achieved a kind of fame, with his photo in the newspapers. When he had called French to tell him about the find, his boss can hardly believe it. Telling Silas to cordon the cabin off, he and the sheriff get there as fast as they can. French is astonished that he had never spotted the cabin himself while searching Larry's land: it had been too well hidden by the kudzu. Silas does not admit how he had found it, but lies, saying he was "[j]ust lucky" (P 211 / K 224).

Silas does not tell anyone that he used to live in the cabin

Agents from the Criminal Investigation Bureau also arrive with their floodlights and forensic equipment, and after half an hour confirm that there is indeed a body buried there. Finally, the smell becomes too much for Silas and he runs outside to vomit. However, he makes himself return to the cabin and watch the removal of the girl's body. She is lying on her stomach, naked, and

It has been confirmed that the Rutherford girl's body is in the cabin

The body has started to decay

her face does not look human anymore. She looks like "something from one of Larry's horror books, black and melted-looking and dissolved" (P 211 / K 225). When he sees her hand, still with red varnish on the nails and her class ring on one finger, he has to go out and be sick again.

Silas wants to stay closely connected to Larry's case

In the meantime, Larry is still lying in a coma, under police guard. Silas asks French if he can take over the night shift outside the hospital room, pretending he needs the extra money. However, the real reason is that he wants to know all the details of how the case is progressing. This is why he has gone out to Larry's house every day since he has been in hospital, even though there is already a police guard there. Silas feeds the chickens every day and collects the eggs, which he gives to Marla at The Hub.

Silas is unsure of his own motivation for protecting Larry now

Every night, he sits outside Larry's room at the hospital, reading the books Larry used to read as a kid. It is not easy to get comfortable, or to stay awake, and Silas has to keep "trying to convince himself of why he was here" (P 214 / K 228). Other patients come to try and catch a glimpse of the alleged murderer. Larry is now the only suspect in the Rutherford case. The media have picked up on the story, and dug up details of Cindy Walker's disappearance. The old cabin has been taken apart in the hope of finding her body, too, but without success. The newspapers speculate that Larry may be responsible for other unsolved cases of missing girls:

The newspapers are convinced of Larry's guilt

> "Maybe these two – and, who knew, others – were buried somewhere on the last acres Larry Ott had refused to sell to the lumber mill." (P 215 / K 229)

Silas is unsure whether he wants Angie to know the truth about him

Silas is mainly worried about Angie, who he has not seen since they had lunch together. She calls him in the evenings to tell him about her day, but he knows that he is deliberately avoiding her. Because she has to work Saturday and Sunday night, he promises to take the Monday off and spend the day with her. He knows then "he'd have to tell her something and worried it might be the truth" (P 216 / K 230). In a way, he wants to open up to her, but is afraid to take that step:

> "He wondered how it would feel to tell her everything, say who he really was, and he worried that if he did, she might start to see him differently." (Ibid.)

Whenever he finds himself falling asleep on his chair, he gets up and walks up and down the hospital corridor. Sometimes he goes into the room and looks at Larry, who, as well as being attached to various machines, is restrained in the bed by leather wrist straps. Although he seems very weak, the doctors say that he is gradually getting better. The news vans have gone from the hospital parking lot for now, but presumably they will return if and when Larry wakes up.

Larry is starting to recover

When he turns up for the night shift, Silas always asks whether Larry has had any visitors, but nobody, apart from the police, hospital staff or the occasional reporter ever comes. On the first evening, Silas unfastens the restraints round Larry's wrists, but they have to be put back on after a nurse complains. At times he hopes that Larry will never recover consciousness. He tries talking to him, but gets no response. He feels the need to warn his old friend about how bad things are going to be for him once he does wake up:

There have been no unusual visitors to the hospital room

Silas is now trying to protect his old friend

> "Don't tell em nothing, Larry, you hear? Hear? They gone try to get you to confess, but don't say nothing, Larry. Hear? Nothing." (P 218 / K 231)

When he is leaving the hospital one day, Jon on the information desk calls him over. He tells Silas that one of the other volunteers reported that Larry had had a visitor on the first day, who had asked if he ever woke up. The man was described as "early twenties, skinny, white" (P 218 / K 232). Silas asks if the man had been caught on the security camera, but Jon tells him it is broken.

A man of Wallace's description has been to the hospital

Silas continues his daily visits to Larry's place. The next time he meets French, he tells him about the 'stringy-looking' visitor at the hospital, but French says that the description is too vague. Then Silas discovers that the sheriff's department has sealed off Larry's house and barn, and he can no longer get to the chickens to feed them. That evening, he buys chicken feed at

Larry's house is now a crime scene and Silas does not have access any more

the supermarket and throws it into the pen. He is able to put down a bowl of water for the hens but has no way of collecting the eggs.

Larry's mysterious visitor returns

One evening at the hospital, when Silas is dozing on his chair, he catches sight of a 'stringy-looking' shadow watching him. By the time he is fully awake, the person is moving away down the corridor. Silas gives chase, but does not manage to catch up with the person.

The nursing home staff are neglecting Mrs. Ott

Having been told that Mrs. Ott is having a good day, Silas finally gets to the nursing home in the afternoon. Brenda tells him Mrs. Ott tried to call her son and became upset when he did not answer his phone. When Silas goes into her room, the first thing he notices is the stink of feces. Mrs. Ott has messed herself and cannot get up to clean herself. Silas goes to fetch the nurse, but Brenda says that the nurses on the next shift will clean her up, in half an hour. Silas wants to know how long she has been lying like that, but Brenda seems barely interested. Silas asks her if this is any way to treat the residents, but this just makes her angry: "Nigger, don't come up in here telling me how to do my job." (P 222 / K 236) She seems to think that Silas is getting ideas above his station, just because his picture has been in the papers recently. Her attitude makes Silas furious. He finds some clean sheets in a cupboard and makes Clyde, the orderly, go and clean Mrs. Ott up. Reluctantly, he obeys, swearing at Silas on his way out.

Silas has to force someone to help Mrs. Ott

He hopes to find out the truth about his mother, but Mrs. Ott is too confused

Now Silas is able to go back into Mrs. Ott's room. She admits that she may have met him before but has forgotten. He introduces himself as a friend of Larry's, but cannot bring himself to tell her what has happened. There is something else that Silas wants to know: he has come to ask Mrs. Ott about his mother. The name Alice Jones means nothing to her, but she recognizes the photo: "Why, that's my boy [...]. And that was our maid" (P 224 / K 238). She remembers that Alice had got pregnant but was not married, so had had to leave her job. She does not remember what happened to Alice after that. Silas asks if she knows who the father of Alice's baby was. Mrs. Ott asks his name again, and says she remembers him as Larry's friend. However, after a while, Silas realizes he is not getting anywhere: "[…] he saw himself come and go in her eyes, she knew him then she didn't." (P 225 / K 239) In the end, he tells her about her chickens until she falls asleep. Before he leaves, he puts the photograph of his mother and Larry in her hand.

There are a few moments when she remembers Silas, but most of the time she is in her own world

When Silas turns up late for his dinner with Angie, she is angry with him. This is the first time they have seen each other all week, yet he has not even called. Silas tries to make the excuse that he is simply tired, but Angie can see that he is lying. She also knows, instinctively, that he did, in fact, date Cindy Walker. Silas remembers how Cindy became his girlfriend. He had often noticed her watching him playing baseball. After a while, he began to do his best to impress her, hitting the ball hard and making daring catches. After one game in which he has played particularly well, he sees her smiling at him and smiles back. It is the first time that she stays until the end of the game. Instead of having a shower, he catches up with her and they start talking. Cindy tells him that she does not like baseball, but comes to the games to see him. Silas is very attracted to her.

The truth about Silas and Cindy

Cindy knows that he comes from Chicago and asks him about it. At first he only talks about baseball, but then, in answer to her questions, he tells her about the snow, about the people in his neighborhood, about traveling on the el train, about the delicious food. She wants to know if they have plays there, like on Broadway, and he tells her yes, his mother had been to see one for her birthday. Cindy dreams, not of being an actress, but of being able to go and see a show. Silas tells her that she could be an actress because she is so pretty:

Cindy wants to know about life in the far-off city of Chicago

> "She gave him a sad smile like he was a simple child. She went on talking, though, said how she couldn't wait to get the hell out of Mississippi […]." (P 230 / K 244)

As they are walking along, a white man in a car slows down and asks Cindy if Silas is bothering her. Cindy shuts him up: "Mind your own business, doofus" (ibid.), and Silas thinks he should go, knowing he would be in trouble with her step-father. Cindy replies scornfully,

A black boy and a white girl together attract unwanted attention

Nobody must find out about their relationship

then asks Silas if he has ever kissed a white girl, leading him to the trees where nobody can see them. From that day onwards, Silas and Cindy secretly become boyfriend and girlfriend, lovers. It is a good time for Silas: he is a baseball star with a promising future and has the excitement of a secret relationship. In a way, he is frightened of continuing to see her, but he cannot resist her.

One day, Cindy tells Silas she first started to like him on the day he had confronted Cecil. Her step-father is always trying to see her naked and would like to have sex with her, especially when he has been drinking. Her mother takes Cecil's side and will not confront him. Cindy has a difficult relationship with her:

> "She, kind of, believes the worst about me. I always been trouble for her. I don't guess I help none, cussing, smoking, messing with boys." (P 231 / K 245)

It seems that Silas takes their relationship more seriously than Cindy does

Silas is not happy that Cindy thinks they are only "messing". One day, Cindy tells Silas that Cecil hit her, saying she was a whore. Cecil will not let her leave the house except to go to school, and has threatened to tell her mother that she, Cindy, wanted to sleep with him. It seems that he knows Cindy is seeing someone and will do anything to keep her away from her boyfriend. Silas himself gets in trouble with his mother: "Son, you got to stop with that white girl." (P 232 / K 246) He tries to deny it, saying they are just friends, but somehow Alice knows the truth. She does her best to warn him: "nothing good ever come out of colors mixing" (ibid.), especially down in Mississippi. Silas retorts that they live in the south because she brought them down here. To placate her, he promises to stop seeing Cindy and concentrate on getting good grades so that he can go to university, but he knows that he does not mean it. It was Cindy who had made the plans to meet up on that fateful weekend, when she would slip out without Cecil noticing and he would take his mother's car.

Silas's mother tries to make him break things off with Cindy

Silas did not know that Cindy had persuaded Larry to bring her to him

Angie has been listening carefully to his story. Silas says he had had no idea that Larry would be the one who drove Cindy to their agreed meeting place, and that she had persuaded him to do so by saying she was pregnant.

He does not think that that was true, but is worried that she might have been. They had spent most of the evening arguing. Cindy had wanted them to run away to Chicago together, but he refused, telling her to go on her own if she wanted to. He had driven her back to the road near her house, where Larry was supposed to meet her again. They were early, and Cindy had jumped out of the car and run down the road. Afraid of meeting a drunk Cecil, Silas had not dared to follow her.

Cindy ran away before Silas could stop her

Once again, Silas had arrived home to find his mother waiting for him. She knew he had disobeyed her and had refused to talk to him. On the following Monday, she had gone into the school to talk to his baseball coach. That was the day that everyone had been talking about Larry and Cindy, about the fact that she had disappeared after their date. Alice arranged for Silas to change schools, to go to Oxford High School and live in his coach's basement. Silas had been relieved at the opportunity to escape from the whole situation in Chabot.

Silas went away to live in Oxford

Angie asks about Larry, and is incredulous when Silas claims to have forgotten about him and Cindy: "You let him take the blame. All this time." (P 234 / K 248) Silas says he thought that Cindy would turn up again, that she had just run away from him on that evening, and that everything would be all right. Angie cannot believe Silas could have thought that for twenty-five years, but he knows that the situation at the time was not that simple:

He justifies his actions at the time; it is only now that he can admit his guilt

> "Things ain't so clear when they're happening, Angie. You're eighteen and playing ball and everything's going your way. Then all of a sudden twenty-five years've passed and the person you look back and see's a whole nother person. You don't even recognize who you used to be. Wasn't till I come back down here that I saw the mess I'd made." (P 235 / K 248f)

The logical conclusion is that Cecil killed Cindy. Both Cecil and his wife are dead now, so there can probably be no proof. He says it might be better if Larry died. Angie is perceptive about his motive: "Better for you?" (P 235 / K 249), and gets him to admit that this is what he

His relationship with Angie has become strained since he told her the truth

believes. However, she knows that Larry is only alive because of Silas, and that things are going to be quite horrendous for him if he regains consciousness. This is the situation that Silas has created, and Angie wants to know what he is going to do about it now.

If Larry dies, it will make things far easier for Silas

That night, in Angie's bed, Silas does not sleep well. The two of them have spent the night together, but, for the first time, not even touching. He goes to the office early, making coffee before going on traffic duty as usual. He drives out to Larry's place, throws more chicken feed into the pen and refreshes the water. He still cannot do anything about the eggs, which have probably started to rot by now. The grass is very overgrown by now, and Silas wishes he could cut it as he once did. If it were possible, he would

Silas would like to change the past, to do the right thing

> "mow his way back to the boy he'd been and do it differently with Larry, go to the police and say, 'She was with me.'" (P 237 / K 251)

He realizes that he lacks the courage to do the right thing. While he is thinking about this, his phone rings. Jon from the hospital is calling to tell him that Larry has woken up.

Chapter Eleven

INFO AT A GLANCE

Larry has woken up in hospital and has to face accusations from the police

- At first, Larry does not know what is a dream and what is reality.
- He discovers that Silas saved his life.
- He reacts violently to the news of how Tina Rutherford died, which makes him seem guilty.
- The police try to make him confess to the crime.

Larry wakes up in hospital, confused. He has been dreaming about himself and Silas sitting in the trees, then sees himself with Wallace. He dreams of the evening in the haunted house when he wore his zombie mask. At one point he catches a glimpse of Silas and hears him say that he should not confess. He sees that he is in hospital. His mouth is very dry and the light hurts his eyes. He drifts in and out of sleep.

He opens his eyes and sees a nurse, who is startled. A man in a blue uniform at the door is talking into a radio. A doctor appears and removes the tube from his mouth, calling for some water for Larry to sip. The doctor starts to check him over. He asks Larry his name and age, and then the name of the president. Larry's first question, however, is "Did they find that girl?" (P 240 / K 253)

The doctor checks whether Larry remembers anything; his first thought is for the missing girl

Larry is feeling a bit better now that the tubes have been taken out of his mouth and nose. There are three men in his room: a doctor, French and another man that he does not recognize. The doctor warns the police officers that Larry is still very weak and will not be able to talk much. He tells Larry that he is lucky to be alive: the bullet just missed his heart. He also reveals that it was Silas who had called for the ambulance, saving Larry's life.

Larry finds out that he owes his life to Silas

French introduces the other man as Sheriff Jack Lolly, and tells Larry they are going to talk to him and record the interview. Trying to move his arms, Larry realizes that he is strapped to the bed. The sheriff starts the interview by asking Larry if he shot himself, but Larry cannot remember, only recalling that Wallace had given him a gun. Sheriff Lolly tells him that the first thing he had done was to ask about Tina Rutherford, which Larry does not remember at first. Instead he remembers his zombie mask and his parents' reaction to it. The doctor points out that it is normal for someone in Larry's situation to be unable to remember everything, but that his memory will return if he relaxes. French wants to know when Larry last saw Tina, but instead Larry asks if she is all right. French tells him exactly what happened to her, and that she was found in his hunting cabin. Horrified, Larry tries to get out of the bed but is held back by the wrist straps. He becomes so agitated that he loses consciousness.

The wrist restaints are a sign for Larry that he has not only been injured; he is also in trouble

He has a violent reaction when he hears what happened to Tina Rutherford

When Larry wakes up again, French and the sheriff are back. The doctor is there too, who tells Larry he can send the police away, if he prefers. But Larry wants to

He is surprised about the things Silas has been doing to help him

talk now. French begins recording again. It seems as if he wants to be kind, telling Larry they want to make things easy for him, and reassuring him that the chickens are being taken care of. He reveals that Silas has been feeding them, and has also been to visit Mrs. Ott, which surprises Larry greatly: "Why [...] would he do all that?" (P 244 / K 258)

French explains that Sheriff Lolly had been a deputy at the time when Cindy Walker disappeared. The sheriff now takes over the interview. First of all, he apologizes for the restraints and takes them off Larry's wrists, saying that the hospital had insisted on them. The sheriff tells Larry that Cindy's disappearance was the biggest thing that had happened at that point in his career. They had not arrested Larry at the time because there had been no proof:

> "Without no body or confession there wasn't any way to prove you killed her. Just what we call circumstantial evidence." (Ibid.)

A friendship between Larry and Silas seems unlikely to French

He repeats what Larry told the police at the time, but implies that he does not believe it. Larry asks to talk to Silas because they used to be friends; French is skeptical about this, saying that it sounded more like the two boys just went to the same school. When Larry insists that they really were friends, French dismisses it: "Okay. We all remember things different, I guess." (P 245 / K 259) French believes that now they have found the cabin, they finally have a reason to convict Larry. The cabin was hidden away, and was on the last bit of land that Larry refused to sell to the mill.

Larry's refusal to sell the land where the cabin is comes across as suspicious

French has a theory about how Larry came to kill the girls, which he now puts across to him. His theory is that, living in a part of the world where everyone knows everyone else's business, Larry became fed up with other people thinking he was a killer. Perhaps he had got to know Tina Rutherford somehow, a young, pretty girl, dressed sexily. Tina might have made contact with him because of his reputation, started to lead him on, pretending to be his "biggest fan" (P 246 / K 260). At first Larry had not reacted to her:

French tries to convince Larry that he killed Tina Rutherford

> "But a man can only resist so long, right, once his rut gets up, and maybe you drank a passel of them Pabst Blue Ribbons we seen in your fridge, or smoked a little dope, got out of your head, and next thing you know you've taken her." (Ibid.)

He suggests that Larry had kidnapped Tina for a bit of companionship, but she had become frightened, perhaps attempted to get away. As a result, and probably without meaning to, Larry had killed her. French believes that Larry then shot himself, out of guilt: "Nothing you meant to do but suddenly it'd done got out of your hands." (Ibid.) He cannot escape what he has done, and so it would be best if he now tells the truth and faces the consequences of his crimes. By now, Larry is starting to believe what the policeman is saying to him:

French's version of the events is very persuasive

> "French talking on in his calm voice, making rape, murder, logical, Larry listening with his veins full of airy drugs and his head afloat, how reasonable if he had done it, strangled the girl and buried her, how these men understood his life so thoroughly" (ibid.).

Larry thinks about what he has been told, that some women almost ask to be raped, and that if you wear a mask, one like his zombie mask, it was as if another person was committing those crimes. With all the pain-killing drugs in his body, Larry almost has an out-of-body experience while listening to French's version of events: he sees himself both as the person in the mask waiting in his house with the gun, and as the person who walked, unsuspectingly, into his house on the day he was shot. Then the two people, "Mask Larry" and "Face Larry" (P 247 / K 261) become the same person and pull the trigger. Larry imagines "how good it would feel to confess, to please these reasonable men doing their reasonable, necessary work" (ibid.).

A mask makes an attacker anonymous, taking away their guilt for the crime

Larry asks French if he thinks he committed the crimes, and French says yes, although he does not know why. Larry cannot imagine why he would have done it either; he did not even know Tina Rutherford, does not know any women except his mother. However, for French, this is not a reason to believe in Larry's innocence: "[S]ometimes we do bad things without knowing the rea-

French brings Larry to the point where he is ready to make a confession

sons" (ibid.). He emphasizes that things are not going to get any better for Larry, and that it would be best for everyone if he simply confesses and takes his punishment. Larry seems to agree.

Chapter Twelve

INFO AT A GLANCE

Silas admits his part in Cindy's disappearance

- Silas rushes to Larry's bedside.
- He admits his part in Cindy's disappearance.
- French questions Silas, but does not want to take the Walker case any further.
- Silas tries to apologize to Larry, but Larry does not accept it.
- Drinking alone in a bar, he meets Irina again and finds out that Wallace probably sent the snake to her mailbox.

Silas hopes he is not too late to stop Larry confessing

At the hospital, Silas hurries up to Larry's room, afraid that French has already 'persuaded' him to confess. Although both the doctor and the police guard on the door try to stop him, he goes into the room, interrupting the interview. Larry is happy to see him. The doctor asks if he wants the police to go away, but Larry does not mind continuing as long as Silas is there. Silas tries to get a few minutes alone with Larry, but French refuses. Larry asks Silas if he has been coming into his room, and Silas admits that he sometimes did. He can only hope that Larry will not say too much before he has had a chance to speak to him alone. He admits that he has been feeding Larry's chickens, and that he was the one who brought Larry a copy of Night Shift. French wants to get back to the subject of Larry's supposed guilt. Silas says Larry should confess "[o]nly if he's done something" (P 251 / K 265), which pleases French even less.

Larry is comforted by Silas's presence

Silas confirms that he and Larry were friends

Larry asks Silas to confirm that the two of them had been friends when they were younger, which Silas does. French wants to get back to the subject of what really happened to Cindy Walker, but Silas intervenes, to French's annoyance, as he feels he is at the point of finally getting a confession from Larry. Larry repeats what he has always said: that he dropped Cindy off at a certain place, as she had asked him to do, and had left her there. French urges him to tell them what happened after that, and at this point Silas steps in: he finally admits he was the one Cindy had gone to see that evening: "I'm the one let her off at her road." (P 252 / K 266) Larry is astonished; French, too, can hardly believe what he is hearing:

Silas confesses he had dropped Cindy off that night

> "You mean [...] he's been telling the truth all this time? And that you, in fact, were the last person to see her alive?" (Ibid.)

Larry asks if Cindy is the reason he went away to Oxford, and also wants to know whether Cindy's, and presumably Silas's, baby had been a boy or a girl. Silas tells him Cindy had not been pregnant after all. He forces himself to look Larry in the eye as he reveals that Cindy had lied, something he had not known back then. He had believed he and Cindy had had a real relationship: "We were in love, or thought we were" (P 253 / K 267). He reveals that he had driven Cindy home earlier than planned, and, because she was angry, she had run off in the dark without waiting for Larry. Both Larry and Silas can clearly imagine the scene when Cindy arrived home, probably in tears, to be confronted by Cecil, drunk and angry. Larry realizes that Cecil must have killed Cindy. The doctor comes back into the room to tell the police they need to leave for today. Sheriff Lolly guides Silas and French towards the door, aware of the tensions between them. Before they go, Larry wants Silas to say that they really were friends, but that is not quite true for Silas:

It is not easy for Silas to admit the truth

After all these years, Larry finds out that Cindy must have been killed by her step-father

> "You were, Larry [...]. I don't know what I was." (P 254 / K 268)

Silas cannot honestly say he behaved like a friend towards Larry

Silas drives behind French and Lolly to the sheriff's department. He feels like a criminal who is about to be interviewed, knowing that French is extremely angry with him. They go into French's small office, and French orders him to start talking.

Silas tells French everything about him and Larry, except that they are half-brothers. French advises him to say nothing. Back in 1982, when Cindy disappeared, he should have come out with the truth. It might even have been possible to convict Cecil Walker of the crime. Now,

Larry has been punished, even though he had nothing to do with Cindy's murder

however, too much time has passed, and Cecil is dead. French understands why Silas did not say anything at the time, but the body has still never been found, and Larry has never been punished for the crime. Silas interrupts this train of thought:

> "Shit [...]. Larry's done time his whole life." (P 255 / K 269)

For French, Larry's innocence in the Walker case does not prove his innocence in the Rutherford case

However, French does not believe it is their job to go into the ethics of what Larry has suffered. He thinks it is best not to remind the public of the Walker case, but instead to concentrate on Tina Rutherford's death. He is sure that the truth will be revealed here if Larry really is innocent. Silas is astonished that French still thinks Larry might have killed Tina: "[...] whoever killed her's probably cashing in on Larry's reputation." (P 256 / K 270) He is sure the real killer deliberately hid the body in the hunting cabin to throw suspicion onto Larry. However, for French this does not prove anything, as very few people knew about the existence of the cabin. As well as this, he believes that Larry had started to confess before Silas turned up. The sheriff agrees with him, and says that Larry has to remain strapped to the bed for the time being. Silas is also told that he is no longer allowed to guard Larry's room.

It is hard for Silas to talk to Larry now that he knows the truth

Silas returns to the hospital. Skip, the officer on guard duty, is surprised to see him and asks him to keep guard outside the door while he has a cigarette. As soon as Skip is out of sight, Silas goes into the room. Larry seems to be asleep, but opens his eyes when Silas says his name. Larry has clearly been thinking about the day's revelations: "All this time people thinking it was me." (P 257 / K 271) Silas apologizes and says they will talk about Cindy another time. Now, however, he wants to make sure Larry is not arrested for the murder of Tina Rutherford, because he knows that Larry is innocent. Larry asks Silas how he can be sure of this, and Silas says he knows, just as he knows that Larry did not shoot himself. Larry is unconvinced of Silas's certainty:

> "How? Cause you knew me for three months, twenty-five years ago? What makes you think you know anything about me now?" (Ibid.)

Avoiding the question, Silas tries to get Larry to say who shot him, thinking that the same person probably killed the Rutherford girl. However, Larry does not answer him. Silas reminds Larry about the message he left just before he was shot, and asks what he had wanted to talk about. When Larry points out that he had never called back, Silas gives the excuse that he did not get the message in time. He also apologizes for never having called back any of the other times that Larry had wanted to talk to him. Larry then says that, the first time, he had wanted to apologize for what he had said to Silas during their fight. Silas forgives him, but Larry feels that perhaps he should take back his apology: "But now [...]. I don't know what to think. Or even if I'm still sorry." (P 258 / K 271) Silas still hopes that Larry might know who shot him, but then Skip returns and makes Silas leave.

Larry cannot forgive Silas for the things he did in the recent past and twenty-five years ago

After this frustrating encounter, Silas goes to the Chabot Bus bar to get drunk. Chip, the bartender, keeps the beers coming. Silas ignores his phone. He thinks back to when he used to ride the bus to school, maybe even this very vehicle before it was converted into a bar. Life had seemed to rush by at that time; now, as a man over forty, he wonders what being an adult really means.

He drinks to forget the events of the day

Silas does not remain alone for very long. A woman comes over to talk to him, and he recognizes her as Irina, who had found the snake in her mailbox. She asks Silas if she can join him, and he agrees, sensing how much trouble he would be in if Angie saw him. Chip brings them both a beer, and when Silas admits that he is drunk, Irina orders a tequila to catch up with him. She tells him she was on her way to a party and had spotted his Jeep outside. It turns out that Irina has some interesting information for him. She has a roommate, Evelyn, who told her about a "weird guy" (P 260 / K 274) she used to go out with. The guy had had lots of guns in his house, and also a lot of live snakes, which he apparently collected. One evening, when he and Evelyn are kissing, she feels uncomfortable with all the snakes in the room and wants to stop, but he refuses. Evelyn threatens to shoot him, but this does not worry him; in fact, she feels he is

The strange man with snakes and guns may be a vital clue

There is evidence that Wallace has acted violently towards women before

almost daring her to do so. Luckily for her, the man does not do anything to her in the end, just tells her to leave. It seems likely that this guy was the one who mailed the snake to them. Evelyn had had to move house because the guy would not leave her alone. Irina then reveals the guy's name: Wallace Stringfellow. Silas is not sure where he has heard the name before, then remembers the man on the four-wheeler that he pulled over. He had noticed the pillowcase the man had with him, and remembers how Larry told him that was a good way to transport snakes.

Silas suspects that Irina has been smoking weed

He resists the temptation to sleep with Irina

Silas tells Irina she had better get to her party while she can still drive. She invites him to come along, but he says that, as a police officer, he "can have a dampening effect for certain kinds of partying" (P 262 / K 276). Instead of going to the party, they have a few more drinks and then drive back to Irina's trailer. Her roommates are out. Silas is very drunk by now, and he asks himself why he has come with her. Irina fetches two more beers and asks Silas to take her boots off. He does so with difficulty, nearly falling over. Irina is clearly expecting to sleep with him, and even in his drunken state he worries about the fact that he is leaving fingerprints everywhere. He thinks of both Larry and Angie, and wonders again what he is doing there. He tells Irina that he has to go.

Chapter Thirteen

INFO AT A GLANCE

Larry realizes who killed Tina Rutherford and decides to tell French

- In hospital, Larry has time to think about his past.
- He remembers that Wallace had come to his house one evening after having done something bad.
- He puts two and two together and realizes Wallace must have killed Tina Rutherford and shot him.
- Larry is no longer prepared to protect his "friends": he does not want to be a victim anymore.

Alone in his hospital room, switching between the different television channels, Larry's head is full of memories. He thinks about all the times his mailbox has been destroyed by teenagers, riding past and knocking it down with a baseball bat. He is tired, not just physically, but generally tired of all the things that have been done to him since Cindy went missing.

Larry has been a victim for years

Larry's heart is beating hard from all the memories. He realizes how much time he has spent just waiting: "this his life, waiting for Silas and Cindy to return" (P 266 / K 279). He thinks back to his date with Cindy, how confident he had felt, how he and his parents had laughed about the story of Cecil Walker trying to swing on the rope: "their last good night" (P 266 / K 280). He remembers the haunted house, how nobody had known that Silas and Cindy were going out. How nobody had spoken to him after he had taken his mask off, and he had had to leave without joining the party. The mask reminds him of Wallace.

The day of his date with Cindy was the last time Larry and his parents were happy

On the local news, he sees that he is still suspected of Tina Rutherford's murder. Larry calls out to the police officer guarding his door. He tells him he wants to talk to Roy French because he has remembered something. Skip tells him that French will not be back until the next day, but Larry decides to wait and talk to him: "Until today, he'd have preferred Silas." (P 267 / K 281) Larry's story is about something that happened shortly after Tina Rutherford disappeared. He had woken up in the middle of the night without knowing why. He goes out onto his porch and finds Wallace sitting there, smoking, "looking very small in the dark" (P 268 / K 281). Without looking at the older man, Wallace says:

Larry has lost his trust in Silas after the day's revelations

Wallace seems to be taking refuge on Larry's porch

> "'I done something.'
> 'What?'
> He didn't say, just inhaled, exhaled his smoke." (P 268 / K 282)

Likewise, he does not respond to questions about where he has been in the last few weeks. Larry tries another tactic, asking him about his dog. The dog is still as aggressive as before, and now Wallace has moved out of his mother's house and is renting his own place near the

Wallace likes to think of himself as someone who does not have to obey the law

catfish farm. He sometimes catches fish in the catfish ponds, as he used to do in the creek on Larry's land when he was a boy. Larry points out that he would be allowed to fish there as much as he likes if he pays for it, but this does not appeal to Wallace: "You know me, Larry. I'm a outlaw. Can't do it legal or it's no fun." (P 269 / K 282)

Larry wants to give Wallace a chance to find something he is good at, just as he was given one

At this point, Larry tells Wallace about his idea that he could become his apprentice. Wallace listens to the suggestion in silence, but does not think it would work because he believes that he is worthless. However, Larry does not accept this. He can understand Wallace's point of view: Larry's own father had always said that he had no talent for mechanical work, and yet in the army he had discovered that he was actually good at it: "Just needed a chance." (P 269 / K 283) Wallace, however, wants to change the subject, asking Larry if anyone has been bothering him recently. Larry has been left in peace for a while now, Wallace being the only person who has been out to his place recently. Larry still thinks of Wallace as a friend: "You never bothered me" (ibid.).

He questions whether any of the friendships in his life have been genuine

During his time in hospital, Larry has been thinking about the friendships he has had. This is why he has decided to tell French what he remembers:

> "Tell how, at first, he'd felt a kind of protection for the man who'd shot him. Who'd been his friend. But he'd thought Silas had been his friend too, hadn't he? Maybe Larry was wrong about the word *friend*, maybe he'd been shoved away from everybody for so long all he was a sponge for the wrongs other people did. Maybe, after all this time, he'd started to believe their version of him." (P 270 / K 283f)

He understands that the innocent world he grew up in has dispeared

Larry has got to the point where he is no longer prepared to defend people who only wish to harm him. He sees how, in Wallace's world, he might even have been a hero to a boy like that. Now Larry can see how the world he grew up in has changed. Most of the trees and plants have gone, cut down. His father had taken a gun to school with him, and had left it in the corner of the room at home where it was always on hand; there was no need to lock it up. He had often been bitten by mosquitoes but they had not carried the diseases that they spread now. He had walked around without a shirt in summer, tanned brown by the sun: nowadays, there was a serious danger of skin cancer. Above all, kids do not just carry guns around anymore: "if you brought a gun to school it was to murder your classmates" (P 270 / K 284). Knowing he cannot protect Wallace anymore, Larry intends to tell French that he knows who shot him and who killed Tina Rutherford. He will provide details of Wallace's life: the beer he drinks, the fact that he was the one who gave Larry the gun he then shot him with, that he seemed to think it was all right to rape girls because they enjoyed it. He will tell French that Wallace confessed to having done something bad, and that he had worn Larry's own zombie mask to shoot him. Above all, Wallace is only one of four people still alive who know about the hunting cabin.

The evidence of Wallace's guilt becomes clear to Larry

Larry decides to stop being a victim, to fight back instead

Larry remembers reading about a way to make mailboxes stronger, so that they cannot be destroyed by vandals, and decides to do this when he leaves hospital. He is tired of being a victim.

Chapter Fourteen

INFO AT A GLANCE

Silas goes to Wallace Stringfellow's house to confront him

- At Larry's house, Silas realizes the driver of the four-wheeler has been back, and wonders if it is the man he stopped on the road.
- He comes across a run-down house on the catfish farm and realizes he has found Wallace's home.
- He talks his way into the house, making Wallace nervous.
- Wallace sets his dog on Silas, which Silas then has to shoot.
- Silas has also been shot and is left bleeding on the floor in Wallace's house.

Silas wakes up the next morning with a terrible hangover, but still just about in time for work. He does not remember everything about the previous evening but is relieved that he woke up in his own bed. Angie had left him two messages during the evening, asking where he was.

Silas feels terrible after his evening of drinking

Alcohol has not helped to ease his guilty conscience

He arrives at Chabot Town Hall at half past seven in the morning and does his usual traffic duty, the noise making his headache worse. Afterwards, he goes into The Hub, and Marla immediately sees what is wrong with him. She brings him a cup of coffee, some food and a bottle of aspirin. He admits that he was drinking because of guilt, but does not want to talk about it: talking does not help. Marla goes off to serve another customer, telling Silas not too be too hard on himself. However, Silas realizes that this is exactly what the problem is: "Letting himself off the hook had been his way of life" (P 273 / K 287).

He realizes he has never taken responsibilty for his past actions

The media will make Larry's life more miserable than ever

At the hospital, he sees three news vans in the parking lot: clearly the news has spread that Larry is now awake. He knows that this is not good, that from now on "it would only get worse for Larry" (P 274 / K 288). He contacts the Sheriff's Department to find out where French is, but he has gone to Oxford for the day to try to arrest the suspect in the M&M case and is not expected to be back until evening.

Silas is determined to prove Larry's innocence

Silas drives out to Larry's place to feed the chickens. He knows very well that French will try again to get Larry to confess to the Rutherford murder. However, with French away, Silas has a day to find evidence of what really happened. He examines the place for anything he might have missed the last time. There is a Pabst beer can lying on the ground. Then Silas spots a new set of tire tracks from a four-wheeler, with the same imprint of a nail that he had found on the mold. Clearly, whoever was driving the four-wheeler has been back; what's more, there are footprints. Somebody has been walking around on Larry's property. After looking for more evidence Silas decides to call on Wallace Stringfellow and ask him whether he had put the rattlesnake in the mailbox.

Someone has returned to Larry's yard since the police had last been there

Silas drives up the hill past the catfish farm. He notices a house, dirty and falling into disrepair, with a satellite dish on the roof and a "mean-looking dog" (P 275 / K 289) tied up outside. The animal does not seem to have any water or shade from the sun. Silas realizes that he can use the dog as an excuse to go inside the house, to investigate the mistreatment of an animal. He wants to see whether the house really is full of snakes. The four-wheeler parked outside seems to be further evidence that Silas has come to the right place, but since there is no name on the mailbox, he radios Voncille to find out who lives there. He is not surprised to hear it is Wallace Stringfellow, and tells Voncille he is going inside to talk to him.

There is a fierce guard dog, like the one Wallace described to Larry

With the dog barking and trying to jump up at him, Silas has to cross the yard carefully. He would like time to examine the tire tracks in the yard, but is aware that the dog is alerting Wallace to his presence. Sure enough, Wallace appears on the porch. Silas keeps his voice casual: "Hey there […]. How you doing?" (P 277 / K 291), but Wallace avoids his eye when he replies. Wallace obviously wants Silas to go away again, but Silas says he just wants to talk to him. Wallace is defensive and tries to stop Silas from entering his house: "What you want to go inside for?" (P 278 / K 291) Silas says he wants to ask him about the dog, inside where it will be quieter. In the end, Wallace has to give in and let Silas inside. The house is an unpleasant place:

Silas does not manage to check the tire tracks before Wallace comes out

> "Silas followed him in, taking a deep, silent breath, not smelling the marijuana or meth he'd hoped to, just beer and cigarettes and filth." (P 278 / K 292)

There are no signs of drug-taking inside the house

There are several aquariums containing snakes. Silas asks whether Wallace collects them, and he says it is his hobby. Silas tries to keep Wallace talking, asking him questions about the different kinds of snakes he has. Now that Silas's eyes have adjusted to the dark room, he notices a zombie mask on a shelf, a mask he has seen before. He asks Wallace where he got it; clearly uncomfortable now, Wallace replies that he does not know. Seeming more and more nervous, Wallace goes outside, Silas following, thinking he is going to run away. However, Wallace has gone over to the dog. Silas calls to him, his hand on his gun, but Wallace says he is just trying to make the dog stop barking. He has untied it and is holding it by its collar, and curses when it bites him.

Larry's zombie mask is on the shelf

Silas has to fight off the dog

By now, Silas is coming towards him. He feels for his radio but it is not on his belt. He warns Wallace again, at which Wallace releases the dog. The animal's reaction is violent: "it was like he'd set off a cannon" (P 280 / K 294). It goes for Silas before he can pull out his pistol, biting his arms and hands. He falls to the ground and struggles with the dog, trying to get hold of its throat while protecting himself from its teeth. In the confusion, he hardly knows what is happening, only that he has to keep fighting.

Silas finally manages to shoot the dog

Suddenly he hears a shot nearby, then another one. He is not sure whether he or the dog has been hit. By now, he and the animal are under the porch. Wallace is yelling at the dog to attack Silas, and Silas tries to use the animal as a shield. There is another shot and he sees Wallace running. It is cold, dirty and smelly underneath the porch. The dog is weakening now, and Silas has managed to get hold of his pistol. He puts it to the dog's head and shoots. He can hear Wallace running around on the porch above his head, firing a gun and yelling "Killed my dog!" (P 281 / K 294)

He shoots Wallace in the leg, but the younger man still gets away

By now, Silas can feel that he has been shot in his left arm and that he is bleeding badly. He manages to crawl to the other end of the porch, emerging just as Wallace comes out of his back door with a long revolver. He does not see that Silas is behind him, aiming his pistol. Silas's first shot misses its target, but he shoots again and manages to get Wallace in the leg. Wallace falls, but is able to get up again and shoots around him, breaking a window. He then escapes into the woods.

Silas is lying injured without any way to call for help

Silas is left lying on the ground, injured and trying to stay conscious. He manages to drag himself into the house to look for a phone, but only finds the base unit. Still bleeding heavily, he stumbles and falls over a table, knocking over one of the aquariums. It breaks and a rattlesnake escapes. He starts to feel very cold and is no longer able to stand, but can only watch as the snake slides past.

Chapter Fifteen

INFO AT A GLANCE

Larry tells French about his relationship with Wallace; French now also believes in Larry's innocence

- French is unable to visit Larry because he is investigating Silas's shooting.
- When he finally arrives, Larry gives him evidence of Wallace's guilt.
- Larry had originally wanted to tell Silas about his suspicions, but decided not to talk to him after finding out the truth about Cindy Walker.
- Larry wonders if he is in some way to blame for the Rutherford girl's death because he had not read the signals from Wallace correctly.

The next morning, when Larry asks, he is told that French is not available to talk to him. Since his wrists are still restrained, he asks the nurse to put the copy of *Night Shift* into his hand so that he can read. In the afternoon, he speaks to Skip, the deputy guarding his door, again, wanting to know when he will be able to meet French: "I got something he'll want to hear." (P 283 / K 296) However, Skip tells him that another crime has been committed and that French is investigating that. Larry asks him to explain further, and he finds out that Silas has been attacked by a dog and shot at a suspect's house. Larry guesses the truth straight away: "Was the fellow, was his name Wallace Stringfellow?" (P 284 / K 296) Skip is astonished, thinking Larry has already seen a report about the incident on television. Larry now feels an even greater urgency to speak to French. Skip calls French on his radio, and brings it to the bed to allow Larry to talk on it. Larry tells him that Wallace was the one who shot him and provides the necessary evidence:

Larry realizes it must have been Wallace who attacked Silas

Larry is finally able to tell French what he knows

> "[…] how Wallace knew of the cabin where they found the girl, his last visit, how Larry had recognized his eyes behind the mask when the fellow shot him, the voice that had asked him to die." (P 284 / K 297)

He describes the mask, then asks French if Silas is okay; French says he will come as soon as he can.

The night, Larry wakes up to the sound of French talking to the guard on night duty. He then comes into the room, carrying "a large plastic bag with what looked like a severed head inside" (P 285 / K 297), which turns

Larry is able to speak to French in person

out to be the zombie mask. He unfastens Larry's wrist restraints and sits down. He asks Larry to identify the mask as his. French tells him that Silas is in recovery after his operation, but it is impossible to say whether he will still be able to use his arm: "That damn pit bull bout tore it off." (P 285 / K 298)

The injuries to Silas's arm may be permanent

French goes on to reveal that the dog is dead, and its head is going to be tested for rabies. He also tells Larry that Wallace is dead, too, but will not say what happened: Larry will need to watch the news to find out. French wants to know about Larry's relationship with Wallace. In the last few days, Larry has had time to see things as they really are:

Larry sees that he befriended Wallace because there was nobody else

> "'I thought he was my friend.'
> 'You got a strange taste in friends.'
> 'I don't know if you noticed,' Larry said, 'but I ain't had a lot of options.'" (P 286 / K 299)

Larry goes on to reflect that, since his mother had moved into the nursing home, French had been his most frequent visitor: "In a way, you were the closest thing I had to a friend till Wallace came." (Ibid.) French does not really show what he thinks about this; instead, he asks for more information about Wallace. Larry's theory is that they were both lonely, which is why Wallace had first started visiting him. He realizes that he had been a kind of father figure for the younger man. Larry tells French that Wallace must have killed Tina Rutherford. When French asks why he did not report this to the police, Larry says that he had tried to, by contacting Silas. He reveals that Silas had then come to see him in hospital, asking if he has any ideas about what really happened. By that time, Larry had worked out that Wallace must have been the killer, but he had not said anything to Silas: "I didn't want to talk to him." (P 287 / K 300) French shows understanding for Larry and Silas: "[…] it strikes me it's long past time the two of yall talked." (Ibid.)

Wallace had looked up to Larry

Larry deliberately did not tell Silas about Wallace

Before he leaves, French fastens Larry's wrist straps again, but says he hopes he will be able to take them off permanently the next day. Then Larry is left alone again with his thoughts. His friendship with Silas is still very much on his mind, how their past experiences are part of the men they are today:

> "[…] time packs new years over the old ones but how those old years are still in there, like the earliest, tightest rings centering a tree, the most hidden, enclosed in darkness and shielded from the weather. But then a saw screams in and the tree topples and the circles are stricken by the sun and the sap glistens and the stump is laid open for the world to see." (Ibid.)

We can suppress our past: but it is always present, deep inside of us

He also thinks about Wallace and wonders whether, in some way, he himself is responsible for Tina Rutherford's death. He realized that, in a twisted way, Wallace had admired him and wanted to copy what he thought Larry had done to Cindy. Larry now regrets "sending him home that night instead of understanding" (ibid.). He also wonders what might have been different if he had spoken to Silas a couple of days ago instead of ignoring him. Perhaps Wallace would still be alive and Silas would not have been injured. While Larry is still thinking about all of this, another patient is wheeled into the room in a bed. It is Silas.

Larry feels he is partly to blame for the murder

Chapter Sixteen

INFO AT A GLANCE

Larry and Silas share a hospital room, giving Silas the opportunity to reveal that they are half-brothers

- Silas wakes up in the hospital room to find Larry watching the TV news.
- The story of the attack and Wallace's death is on the news.
- Silas tells Larry that they are half-brothers; in a way, Larry has always known.
- Silas had longed for a father whereas Larry had been miserable growing up with one.
- Larry does not want to remain in the same room as Silas.

Silas wakes up on his back in the bed next to Larry's. Not noticing that Silas is awake, Larry is once again clicking through the channels on the television. In Silas's imagination, this could have been reality for the two of them, that they could have been "normal brothers all the years of their rearing, both black or both white, sleeping side by side in matching twin beds" (P 289 / K 301). Things, of

Silas now feels a connection to Larry as his brother

course, did not work out that way, and now they are lying in one room like strangers.

He is lucky not to have been more seriously injured

The only light in the room comes from the TV. Silas carefully moves his injured arm which, all being well, will heal almost completely, although he will have to undergo a lot of physiotherapy. After his surgery, he had asked to be put into the same room as Larry, and was a little surprised when French agreed.

Larry has now found a local news channel and is watching a report about the attack on Silas. The image from the attack that sticks most clearly in Silas's mind is the zombie mask, with its connection to the past:

Silas could have let Larry feel included on the one evening he'd felt he belonged

> "How different would their worlds have been if he'd followed Larry across the road toward his mother's Buick way back when, that long-ago haunted house? What if he'd just reached out and took Larry's shoulder, said, 'Wait'?" (P 290 / K 302)

The anchor goes on to say that it was Voncille, becoming worried when she had been unable to contact Silas on her radio, who had sent two police cars to check out Wallace's place. The police officers had found him, unconscious and bleeding, with a rattlesnake nearby. They had managed to capture the snake and Silas was taken to hospital. In the meantime, Wallace had run into the woods, followed by the police deputies. Shots had been fired on both sides, and then Wallace had apparently shot himself dead. The deputies had searched the property and, as well as drugs, had found Tina Rutherford's wallet. French also appears in the report, but refuses to say in front of the camera whether Larry has now been cleared of any involvement in the murder.

Wallace killed himself before the police could arrest him

At first, Larry does not seem prepared to listen to Silas

Silas presses the button that moves his bed so that he can get into a more upright position. Larry mutes the TV and tells Silas: "You're a hero" (P 292 / K 303). Silas tries to start a conversation, but Larry turns back to the television and switches the sound on again. For Silas, the time has come to have a serious talk with Larry, but he has "no idea where to begin" (ibid.). Larry ignores Silas's request to switch off the TV while they talk. This is not ideal, but Silas realizes that he can just talk anyway, since Larry cannot get up and walk away.

Gradually, Larry focuses more on what Silas is saying, switching off the television and sitting motionless in his bed. Silas tells him everything he has found out about their real relationship in the last few days, and is left emotionally exhausted by the time his has finished his story:

It is not easy for Silas to tell Larry about their father

> "Silas felt flattened by the truth, or the telling of it, his lungs empty and raw and the spaces behind his eyes throbbing." (P 292 / K 304)

When he says that they are brothers, Larry corrects him: "Half brothers." (Ibid.) Silas then asks Larry if he knew; Larry's first response is that he did not, but then has to admit that, on some level, he had known ever since the first morning his father had stopped to give Silas and his mother a ride. Larry's mother giving them coats had been another hint. As well as this, Larry guessed what his father thought of the situation: "He wished you'd been the white one" (P 293 / K 304). Silas thinks back to the day that Mrs. Ott gave them the coats. He put his on straight away, glad of the warmth, but Alice just stood there looking at it, then started to carry it back to the cabin as if it was something horrible. Silas asks her if she is going to put it on, not able to understand her reluctance. However, after a while Alice gives in, puts the coat on and buttons it up:

In a way, Larry had guessed the truth

Carl preferred a son like Silas to one like Larry

> "Silas had followed her, still not seeing what an emblem of defeat, shame, loss, hopelessness, the coat was." (P 293 / K 305)

For Alice, accepting the coat meant sacrificing her dignity

Now, as an adult, he can see how his lack of understanding as a boy has affected the kind of man he is today. Larry asks if Silas thinks his life was better, living with Carl, and Silas has to admit that life was probably not easy for Larry. However, he says that it also was not easy growing up without a father, and that he had used to envy Larry, wishing he too had lots of land, guns and a warm place to live. Larry seems scornful when he hears this: "Bet you don't wish it now" (ibid.). Silas cannot think of an answer, and before he can say any-

It is hard to say who was worse off: Larry growing up with a father or Silas growing up without one

thing else, Larry presses the buzzer by his bed and asks the nurse that comes in if he can be moved to another room.

Chapter Seventeen

INFO AT A GLANCE

Larry is still refusing to talk to Silas

- Being popular, Silas has a lot of visitors.
- Angie has forgiven Silas for the way he has treated her; she also shows sympathy and understanding towards Larry.
- French tells the two men that Larry's name has been cleared.
- There are lots of television news teams that want to talk to Silas and Larry.
- Silas leaves hospital; Larry decides not to change rooms.

Angie has forgiven Silas, relieved that he is okay

Unlike Larry, Silas has a lot of visitors while he is in hospital. The first one is Angie, who smiles at Larry as she passes his bed. Since Larry has asked the nurse to pull the curtain across between the two beds, he can only hear them talking. Silas apologizes to Angie for the way he has been behaving, but she has forgiven him. She is relieved she had not been called to the crime scene to pick up the injured Silas: "She didn't know what she'd have done, something happened to him." (P 295 / K 306) When they start to talk more quietly, Larry is sure they are talking about him. As usual, he is watching television, with the sound on low. There is only one TV in the room, and, although Silas has his own remote, "Larry maintained control" (P 296 / K 306).

She shows sympathy for Larry

She offers him a way to start going to church again

After a while, Angie introduces herself to Larry as Silas's girlfriend. He realizes that she is the one who found him, and thanks her for that, even though she emphasizes that it was Silas who sent her. Angie goes on to tell Larry she is sorry for everything that he has suffered, and that he would be welcome at her church if he wants to go there. Knowing it is a black church, Larry is not sure how to respond to this offer, eventually asking if Silas goes there, too. However, Angie tells him that Silas never voluntarily goes to church. She stays in their room for most of the night, but is gone the next morning.

Silas's next visitor is Voncille, who has brought him flowers. He thanks her for saving him by sending the deputies to check up on him. Later, the mayor of Chabot turns up and jokes with Silas about going back to work with his injured arm. A couple of deputies drop in and tell Silas what happened to Wallace's snakes. They have all been taken away as evidence, except for one boa constrictor nobody had noticed: it suddenly appeared and had to be shot. They give Larry a friendly nod as they leave.

Silas gets a lot of praise for his actions

French turns up, smartly dressed in a shirt instead of his usual T-shirt. He stands at the end of the curtain between the beds so that he can see both patients at the same time. He tells Silas that the attractive anchorwoman from the news wants to talk to him, but Silas asks him to release Larry from the restraints before he does anything else. He does so with an apology. Larry rubs his sore wrists and starts watching TV again. French pulls the curtain back, asking Larry to switch off the television as he wants to talk to the two of them.

French starts by telling them that, as well as Tina Rutherford's wallet, they found eleven firearms, ammunition and drugs at Wallace's house. The zombie mask has now been examined and a trace of Larry's blood has been found on it, proving that Wallace was the one who shot Larry. Because of what Larry told them about where Wallace got his drugs, they had also decided to re-examine the murder of M&M. French now thinks they will discover the Wallace also killed M&M.

There is now little doubt that Wallace shot Larry

After these revelations, French goes on to say that several television news teams are interested in interviewing the two of them. French does not see any reason to remain silent now that things have been cleared up. Now that they know the truth, Tina Rutherford's parents "send their apologies to Mr. Ott" (P 298 / K 309), and also wish to thank Silas. Soon after French's visit, Silas is discharged from hospital, promising to come and visit Larry. The nurse comes along to take Larry to his new room, but he decides to stay where he is.

Silas and Larry have become local celebrities

Chapter Eighteen

INFO AT A GLANCE

Silas starts trying to make amends for the way he has treated Larry

- The only interview Silas will give is to the local police reporter, who he has been avoiding.
- The mayor wants Silas to take on more real police work.
- Larry is still refusing to talk to him.
- Silas and Angie clean Larry's house, and Silas returns the rifle.

Silas decides not to talk to the big media outlets

Angie drives Silas to the town hall. He is still in a lot of pain and feeling very tired, but he is happy to have left the hospital. Earlier that day, he had given an interview to Shannon, the local police reporter who has been trying to reach him for days. He wants her to have exclusive rights to the story, rather than one of the big networks like CNN. She asks if Larry will confirm the story, but Silas says she will have to ask him herself.

At first it is not clear what the mayor wants to tell him

Silas knows that Angie is happy now that she gets to look after him for a few days. He goes into the town hall to find the mayor and Voncille waiting for him. Silas wants to speak first, but the mayor interrupts him, joking about the way he has been neglecting his job recently. He and Voncille have clearly planned what they are going to say to him: when he asks Voncille what they should do with Silas now, she replies: "You could fire him [...]. But who'd you get to replace him on that salary?" (P 301 / K 311) Instead of this, the mayor is planning to hire a part-time officer to do jobs like directing the traffic, leaving Silas free to do "real police work" (ibid.). This has been approved by Mr. Rutherford, who has even suggested that Silas might be given another car. For a few moments, Silas hardly knows what to say. He is very grateful, but he tells them:

Silas is going to be rewarded rather than punished

> "[...] I can't take none of it. Not yet. You got to wait till the paper comes out." (P 302 / K 311)

He is not very comfortable with going to visit Larry, but feels that he should do so

Angie enjoys taking care of Silas, even bringing him dinner in bed. In the evening, they watch movies together; when Silas wakes up in the night, he cannot help thinking about Larry. The next day, he gets Angie to drive him to Larry's house to collect his mail, and then take him to the hospital. Silas is nervous seeing to Larry, unsure of what he should say to him. However, Angie reassures him that he does not have to talk to Larry at all: "Just go and sit with him. See what happens." (P 302 / K 312)

In the hospital room, Larry is still doing his best to ignore Silas. He refuses to look at the box of mail Silas has brought. Silas makes a few attempts to get Larry to talk, telling him that he is still feeding the chickens, and that somebody will need to come and cut Larry's grass as he is unable to do it at the moment. After about an hour, Silas gives up and leaves, promising to come back the next day.

Silas tries to bring his friendship with Larry back to life

Silas also goes to see Larry's mother again. He is still in pain, and the plaster cast on his arm is very heavy. Although his arm hurts so much, he has stopped taking painkillers:

Since no-one else has punished him, Silas is punishing himself

> "He didn't fool himself: the pain was penance. Were his visits to Mrs. Ott more penance?" (P 303 / K 313)

He tries to chat to her, recalling memories of the one special day he'd spent with Larry and telling her about it. However, Mrs. Ott has no idea who he is and cannot understand what he is telling her. Later that day, he revisits the Walkers' house. It is now covered in vegetation, which gives it "another layer of mystery" (P 304 / K 313). Looking up at the window of what had been Cindy's room, he wonders whether the house is haunted by her ghost.

Nobody knows what really happened at the Walker place

On the following day, Silas and Angie drive out to Larry's house. Silas pulls the police seals down. Angie has brought cleaning supplies, and starts scrubbing the blood off the floor. Silas takes the old catalogs and other junk mail out of the gun cabinet and puts them on the kitchen table. He then fetches the rifle he won from Larry in the fight. With Angie's help, he has cleaned it. He lifts it as if he is about to fire it, admiring the way it looks, how well it is made. Doing so awakens more memories for him:

Silas wants Larry to have a fresh start when he gets out of hospital

> "Holding it for a moment he was a boy again, the world the world it had been a long time ago, a world full of unknowns, a world full of future and possibility [...]." (P 304 / K 314)

Silas gives back the rifle

Carefully, he places the rifle in the gun cabinet: "a thing returned to its rightful place" (P 305 / K 314). Now that he is a man, Silas realizes that the world is still as uncertain as it was back then, but that there is hope for his future. Part of that hope is Angie.

Chapter Nineteen

INFO AT A GLANCE

Silas and Larry make the first steps towards rekindling their friendship

- Larry enjoys Silas's visits but does not feel the need to speak to him.
- One night he gets up and walks out of the hospital.
- The hospital volunteer notices and calls Silas, who goes to look for him.
- Silas finds Larry walking along the road and drives him home.
- Larry tells Silas to bring his Jeep over the next day so that he can repair it.

Larry does not feel he owes it to Silas to talk to him

Silas has visited Larry for the last four days, but Larry has not spoken to him. He is pleased to see Silas and glad to realize his old friend's nervousness, but does not feel any pressure to talk to him:

> "Not talking was easy when you had no idea what to say and, he supposed, it was his right." (P 306 / K 315)

Along with the mail, Silas has brought him some clothes and boots. Larry realizes that Silas must have been in his house, looking through his belongings. Silas reassures Larry that the chickens are doing well, and that his mother is no better and no worse.

He is finally allowed to leave his hospital room

Five days after Silas was discharged, the doctor examines Larry and tells him his wounds are healing well. He should, however, take better care of himself, eat more healthily and get more exercise. The doctor gives him permission to leave his room and walk around the hospital corridors. As before, the doctor is sympathetic towards Larry and what he has been through: "[...] I'm glad it seems to be over now." (P 307 / K 316) Larry asks when he can go home, and the doctor says probably in two or three days. Larry rings for the nurse, who helps him out of bed, and he walks along the hospital halls. He cannot help wondering whether his nightmare is really over. He takes the elevator to the lobby on the ground floor and looks at all the news vans and reporters, waiting outside to interview him. None of them notice him, and he gets back into the elevator before one of them does.

He finds it hard to believe his ordeal is over

At ten o'clock that night, a time when there are hardly any nurses around, Larry gets up and takes the elevator back down to the lobby. He has nothing except the clothes he is wearing, and regrets not asking French for his keys, wallet and phone. He has lost weight while in hospital and has to make his belt tighter. In the lobby, he hears someone cough in the gift shop, although it is closed, which makes him put his head down and walk out as fast as he can. He hopes the volunteer at the information desk has not had a chance to get a good look at him, and goes outside.

Larry leaves the hospital without telling anyone

There are no reporters outside at this time of night: presumably they have gone to the motel. Larry crosses the parking lot, wishing he had a cap as the night is cool. He starts walking towards Fulsom, although it is at least two miles away. Larry realizes that walking there will not be easy, imagining the neighborhoods he will have to go through, "kids standing in the yards to watch him pass, dogs barking on their leashes" (P 308 / K 317). However, he does not have any choice, as there are no local taxi services and he does not have any money with him to rent a car. His aim is to get to his shop, although it is a long walk away.

He wants to walk to his shop, where he will be safe

Larry is still wondering whether his days as "Scary Larry" are really behind him now. Before leaving the hospital, he had watched a news report that confirmed everything French had told him: Wallace had committed suicide and was now seen as Tina's Rutherford's killer. Due to his gunshot wound, Larry finds it hard to walk, and before long he is sweating heavily. His chest starts to hurt, but he keeps going.

He does not know if he will ever escape his reputation as Scary Larry

Silas is alone at Angie's house while she is on night duty. His cell phone rings: Jon, the volunteer at the hospital, is calling to tell him that Larry has just walked out of the hospital, although he has not been officially discharged. Silas gathers a few necessary items and gets into his Jeep, which is parked outside Angie's apartment. As usual, it takes a few moments for the old car to start. Silas has found a way to drive using just his good hand, using his knee to steer. It is not very comfortable, but it works. He drives past the hospital, along the road that Larry must have taken.

Silas sets off in his Jeep to look for Larry

Sure enough, before long he spots his old friend limping down the street. He pulls over and asks Larry if he wants a ride. Larry does not answer, but gets into the Jeep. Silas offers to take him back to the hospital, but Larry wants to go home. They drive in silence for a while. Silas gives Larry the bottle of water he has brought with him, and Larry drinks it. They pass through the town center, empty of people, past the strip malls and out into the countryside. It takes a while for Larry's breathing to get back to normal. When he finally speaks, it is to ask Silas about the Jeep, guessing what model it is. He tells Silas that he can hear the carburetor needs to be repaired. Silas remembers driving slowly like this with Cindy:

Larry allows Silas to drive him home

> "[…] not wanting to let her go, say good night. On those nights he'd wanted to hold on to her forever." (P 311 / K 320)

Silas's memories of Cindy are still strong

Silas turns onto the gravel road that leads to Larry's house. They drive past the Walker place, now hidden behind the layers of weeds and vegetation: "The land had a way of covering the wrongs of the people." (P 312 / K 320) Silas asks if he can bring the Jeep to the shop for Larry to fix, but Larry says he might not be reopening for a while. They stop outside the Ott house and Larry gets out, thanking Silas for the ride. Silas then hands over the bag containing Larry's keys, wallet and phone.

The crimes committed at the Walker place are starting to fade to memories

Larry walks slowly towards his house, then stops and turns. He tells Silas he can bring the Jeep over to the house tomorrow and he will take a look at it there. Silas says he will. With difficulty, Larry climbs the steps to his porch and lets himself into the house. Just by looking at him from behind, Silas can tell how astonished he is to see that his house has been cleaned and polished. There are flowers on the table, a basket of fruit and scented candles in the room. Angie and Silas have put food in the refrigerator and had satellite television installed. Silas has even found a way to drive the tractor with one hand, and has been able to move the chickens around onto fresh grass. He has collected the eggs for Larry, too.

Larry's house is like new, and full of surprises prepared by Silas and Angie

Silas drives away again through the "country dark" (P 313 / K 321), so different from the bright lights of the city. Silas feels at home here now. In his house, Larry sits for a while, then gets up and discovers the rifle in the gun cabinet. Slowly, he walks through the house, switching off the lights, and gets into bed. His last thought before falling asleep is that he will have to call Silas in the morning and tell him to buy a carburetor kit so that he can repair the Jeep.

The return of the gun is a way for Silas to ask for forgiveness

2 Analysis and Interpretation

Note on the Language

INFO AT A GLANCE

The characters speak in the dialect of the deep south
- Words and grammatical structures are shortened.
- Auxiliary verbs are often left out.
- Unusual past participle forms are used.
- Dialect words are used.

The language and grammar used in *Crooked Letter, Crooked Letter* reflect the way that people in rural Mississippi speak. Below are some examples of the English used.

Auxiliary verbs are missed out, especially in questions:
- "How you know that?" (P 29 / K 46) = *How do you know that?*
- "We at Larry Ott's house like you said?" (P 37 / K 55) = *We are at Larry Ott's house like you said.*

Use of the third person present:
- "You know he do everything I tell him" (P 160 / K 175) = *You know he does everything I tell him.*

Use of the verb 'to be':
- "maybe you wasn't there then" (P 140 / K 155)

Use of 'gone' instead of 'going to':
- "You gone see Roy today?" (P 107 / K 123) = *Are you going to see Roy today?*

Use of 'a' instead of 'have' in certain structures:
- "he'd a never scaled that tree" (P 141 / K 157) = *he would never have scaled (climbed) that tree*

Use of the past participle instead of the simple past:
- "I seen you was in the paper" (P 159 / K 174) = *I saw that you were in the paper.*

Use of 'done' instead of 'had':
- "She'd done saved enough money for a house trailer"

(P 163 / K 178) = *She had saved enough money for a house trailer.*

Dropping of 'if' in conditional sentences:
- "I had me a gun I could kill some of these squirrels" (P 60 / K 77) = *If I had a gun, I could kill some of these squirrels.*

Use of 'ain't' to replace the verb 'to be':
- "I ain't riding up there" (P 121 / K 137) = *I am not riding up there*
- "Ain't you hungry?" (P 126 / K 141) = *Aren't you hungry?*

Use of personal pronouns instead of reflexive pronouns:
- "soon as I get me a job" (P 126 / K 142) = *as soon as I get myself a job*

Use of double negatives:
- "I ain't never hurt nobody in my life" (P 206 / K 220) = *I've never hurt anybody in my life*

Use of dialect words, abbreviated forms and contractions:
- naw = *no*
- yall = *you*
- preciate it = *I appreciate it* (often used to thank someone)
- borry = *borrow*
- hon = *honey* (as a term of endearment)
- em = *them*
- set = *sit*
- thunk = *thought*
- brung = *brought*
- dranking = *drinking*
- bout = *about*
- ever body = *everybody*
- ole = *old*
- cept = *except*
- outta = *out of*

The novel also contains a lot of typical botanical, mechanical and baseball terms. For further information see the annotations and glossary in the Klett English edition (Stuttgart: Ernst Klett Sprachen, 2017).

Characters

Larry Ott

INFO AT A GLANCE

"Scary Larry" is an outsider who just wants to be accepted

- Larry's unusual hobbies make him a misfit.
- He finds it hard to judge whether people really want to be friends with him.
- His loneliness leads him to misjudge Wallace.
- At the end of the novel, he wants to change his passive life.

Larry was not a strong, healthy boy that his father could be proud of

Larry Ott has always been an outsider, even as a child. He and his parents lived in a remote place, with few neighbors, making it difficult for him to meet up with other kids when he is not at school. As a child, he was often ill, suffering from asthma, hay fever and allergies. He had to wear glasses, which often got broken. To his father's disappointment, Larry has not inherited his "tall, pitcher's physique" (P 45 / K 62), but rather the "shambling, stoop-shouldered pudginess" (P 44 / K 61) typical of his mother's side of the family. To make matters worse, he had started to stutter when he was in the second grade, making reading out loud at school a miserable experience for him:

He was teased and bullied by the other kids, even from a young age

> "When he stuttered the other boys laughed and his teacher thought he was doing it on purpose and fussed at him." (P 97 / K 114)

In addition to this, Larry does not have the same interests as most boys of his age. He is an avid reader, especially of horror stories, while most boys prefer sport. Furthermore, Larry is interested in nature. He likes fishing, but also catches animals like snakes and keeps them in the barn. He knows a lot about reptiles, and nature in general, but Silas is the first person who has ever been interested enough to listen to him. For most of the kids at school, however, Larry's interests just make him seem weird:

> "He use to bring stuff to school, snake's he'd catch, trying to make people notice him." (P 163 / K 178)

Larry has always wanted friends but does not know how to make the other boys like him, so has resorted to trying to get their attention in other ways. One Halloween, he comes to school with a zombie mask and is invited to play an active role at a haunted house party later that day. He does so with great success, and clearly hopes that the other kids of his age will now include him, make him part of their group. However, he cannot shake off his reputation of being an outsider, and the others simply ignore him. Lacking the courage to go over and join them of his own accord, Larry is left with no choice but to drive home alone.

Larry wants attention, but does not seem to realize it will not help him make friends

Larry is very naive, and this naivety leads him to make some bad choices. Believing that two boys in his class, Ken and David, will let him go to the drive-in movie with them, at their instigation he insults one of the black girls at the school. Naturally, when he gets beaten up by the other black kids afterwards, Ken and David do not come to his aid:

He is naive: he takes people at face value, even when they are just laughing at him

> "Some part of him hoped the white boys would rally for him, admire him for what he'd said, but they were laughing and pointing at him […]." (P 57 / K 75)

Likewise, he genuinely believes that Cindy wants to go on a date with him, since she is the one who asks him out: he would never have dared to ask someone like her for a date. Having no experience with girls, he cannot read the signs, in the days leading up to the date, that Cindy is not, in fact, interested in him. He goes to look for her at school near the sports field, to tell her about the movie that is showing on Friday evening. Clearly not wanting to talk to him in front of her friends, Cindy comes over to Larry, but is not interested in what he has to say, hardly seeming to understand what he means. He notices Silas "staring at the two of them" (P 135 / K 150), but obviously cannot guess the real reason for this, perhaps thinking he is making Silas jealous. The fact that he even wonders "if he should take Cindy fishing on their second date" (P 135 / K 151) shows how completely he has misjudged the situation.

He does not suspect that Cindy may have an ulterior motive

Cindy is only using Larry

Larry is someone who is easy to manipulate, and Cindy takes advantage of that. She appeals to him for help to get away from her step-father, adding that she is pregnant to make it even more emotional: "You the only person in the world who can help me, Larry." (P 148 / K 163) Larry has no idea how to get out of this situation, and is left with no option but to agree. Later that night, when Cindy does not turn up at their agreed meeting place, he is even more helpless, with no idea how to react. However, he initially keeps his promise not to tell anyone about Cindy's baby, which gets him into even deeper trouble: it seems to the police that, if he lied about this, he was probably lying about the other events of the night, too. Larry's attempt to protect Cindy leads to his downfall.

Larry only wanted to protect Cindy: instead, he ends up taking the blame

In the aftermath of Cindy's disappearance, Larry's reputation works against him. Already marked down as a weird misfit, he now becomes known as "Scary Larry". Although no evidence is ever found that he harmed her, the police presume he is guilty of killing Cindy, and do not even appear to look for any other suspects. Likewise, when Tina Rutherford goes missing, he is immediately suspected, although, again, there is no evidence that he even knew her.

By this time, Larry seems to have accepted that he will never change other people's opinion of him: he understands why French searches his house for evidence that he killed the Rutherford girl. He is almost passive about it by now, allowing French to search his house without even reading the search warrant. His empathy even extends to his attacker, because he knows from personal experience that "all monsters were misunderstood" (P 8 / K 24). This does not mean that Larry considers himself to be a monster, but he knows that other people see him as one, without knowing what he is really like.

He feels empathy with monsters because that is how other people see him

It is a combination of naivety and desperate loneliness that leads to Larry's friendship with Wallace. Until Wallace starts to visit, the only people who have been near Larry's house, apart from French, are drunk teenagers who had come to damage his property and intimidate him. During Wallace's first visit, Larry remains polite as always, uncertain of the younger man's motive for coming out to his place. On his subsequent visits, Larry is still wary of Wallace at first, leading Wallace to believe that Larry does not like him, but gradually he gets used to having the other man around. At one point, he even makes Larry smile spontaneously, something he has not done for years. Wallace tells Larry that they are similar in many ways, but Larry becomes aware that their attitudes towards many things are quite different. Wallace is a heavy drinker, and smokes weed, neither of which Larry would ever do. Furthermore, Wallace clearly has a violent streak, implying that he would rape a woman if he got the opportunity, something Larry would never dream of doing. However, Larry sees the good side even of someone like Wallace, and imagines saving him from himself: training him to be a mechanic and take over his shop one day, thinking having a purpose in life would keep Wallace "on the straight and narrow" (P 208 / K 222). Although Wallace is clearly disturbed, Larry ignores the signs, which ultimately lead to his attack.

Wallace is the first friend Larry has had since Silas

He does not realize that he cannot help Wallace

Discovering the truth about what happened to Cindy Walker is a turning point for Larry, causing him to reassess several aspects of his life. Up until then, he had felt guilty for the way his and Silas's friendship ended, and had even tried to contact Silas to apologize. However, everything changes when he learns that Silas is indirectly to blame for everything he has suffered since the night of Cindy's disappearance, because he had never come forward with the truth: "All this time people thinking it was me." (P 257 / K 271) He realizes that he is exhausted by the life he has been forced to lead:

Silas effectively ruined Larry's life

> "He was tired. Even though all he'd been doing was sleeping, he'd never been so tired." (P 264 / K 278)

Larry sees now that Wallace was not really his friend, and, although he had wanted to protect the younger man at first, he cannot do that anymore: he needs to tell the police what he knows. Wallace had pretended to be his friend, but in fact there was no real connection between them. The time has come for Larry to stop being passive, and actively save himself from prison, possibly

Learning the truth about the past allows Larry to see the truth about the present

even execution, for a crime he did not commit. At the end of the novel, he takes positive steps towards taking his life back into his own hands: he leaves the hospital in the middle of the night and heads for home, where he can live the way he wants to. He also appears to accept Silas's attempts to repair their friendship by offering to fix his Jeep. Although Larry wonders if people really will see him differently and treat him better from now on, there are signs that he and Silas, at least, will be able to renew their friendship.

Silas Jones

INFO AT A GLANCE

Silas is the local police constable who has to come to terms with his past

- He takes risks, e.g. when he defends Cindy against her father.
- Up until now, he has lied to himself about the significance of certain events in his past.
- He is forced to admit his guilt and responsibility for what has happened to Larry.
- He has to work for Larry's forgiveness.
- It is a shock to discover the father he has always longed for is, in fact, Carl Ott.
- He comes to realize how badly he treated his mother.

He has to give up his dream of being a baseball player

Silas Jones is the "sole law enforcement" (P 9 / K 26) in the small town of Chabot and the surrounding area. He is often known as "32", the number of his shirt back when he was a star baseball player; however, due to an injury, he never turned professional. He joined the navy, then spent ten years in Oxford after graduating from police academy, but returned to Chabot, near where he went to high school, to take on the job as constable.

He takes a great risk in challenging Cecil

Although he can generally be seen as a positive character, there are some contradictions in his behavior. On the one hand, he is not afraid to stand up for what is right. As a teenager, he shows great courage when he confronts Cecil Walker, who is humiliating Cindy in front of Carl Ott. The fact that he is a black boy yelling at a white man makes this even more shocking: Cecil and Carl are "speechless at his appearance" (P 93 / K 110).

However, on the night he dropped Cindy off after their last meeting, he does not dare follow her to the house knowing that Cecil is likely to be waiting. It is understandable that he does not want to risk meeting Cecil on this occasion, as there is no knowing what the older man might have done to him. This will, however, prove fatal for Cindy as, left to face her step-father alone, she was presumably killed no long afterwards.

Silas's past is a burden he has had to carry for many years, and yet he is not always honest with himself about it. He tells Angie that, after he left Chabot, he had forgotten all about Larry and Cindy:

He has lied to himself about past events

> "It wasn't hard. I was busy in Oxford, and Momma, in her letters, she never mentioned it." (P 234 / K 248)

He says he had always presumed that Cindy would just turn up again at some point and everything would be okay. Angie does not buy this: "For twenty-five years, you thought that?" (P 235 / K 248) Silas makes the excuse that he had been very young then, with a good life and a successful baseball career ahead of him, and had not realized the consequences of his actions until much later: "Wasn't till I come back down here that I saw the mess I'd made." (P 235 / K 249) This admission of his guilt is the first step towards making amends.

Angie forces him to face the truth

As the investigation into Tina Rutherford's murder progresses, Silas's guilty conscience gets the better of him. He admits to himself that he has avoided taking responsibility for his actions: "Letting himself off the hook had been his way of life." (P 273 / K 287) The time has come to step up and do the right thing, which he does by confessing the truth about Cindy's disappearance, thereby clearing Larry's name. However, when it becomes clear that French still believes Larry to be guilty of the Rutherford killing, Silas realizes he has a further responsibility towards Larry to find the real killer. In the process, he nearly gets killed himself, but accepts the pain in his arm as part of his punishment. He is aware that, although for years he acted as if Larry had betrayed him, his own actions have done far more damage. Despite Larry's initial rejection of his attempts to make up for

He knows he has to take responsibility for the past

He needs Larry's forgiveness before he can move on

what he had done, Silas keeps visiting him, visiting Mrs. Ott and taking care of his chickens. It is a great relief when Larry seems willing to forgive him after all. Finally, it seems, he will be able to put the past behind him and look to the future.

Silas has longed for a father

Silas had grown up without knowing who his father was. When he and his mother are traveling south, he asks whether his father is one of the people she knows there. Instead of answering, Alice warns him: "Don't be asking so many questions." (P 117 / K 132) Later, when Carl demands to know who his father is, Silas replies that he is dead. It is not until he finds the photo of his mother with baby Larry on her lap that he realizes the truth: Alice had been the Ott's maid, and Carl must have got her pregnant and then sent her away to Chicago. Even with this evidence, he cannot quite believe it. His visits to Mrs. Ott are not purely out of compassion; he also hopes to find out the whole truth by showing her the photo. Ina has a clear moment when she is able to identify Larry and Alice in the picture, but then her mind goes blank again. She is not capable of connecting Silas with the woman in the photo.

Having no experience of fathers, even someone like Carl seems better than nothing for Silas

Carl does not seem like the kind of person a boy would be happy to have as a father, and yet, for Silas, even he would have been better than no father at all. On the one afternoon he spends at the Ott's place, he takes great pleasure in cutting the grass, and does a very good job. Of course, he has to disappear before Carl gets home and sees him there. Carl praises Larry, thinking he is the one who did the job. Overhearing this, Silas becomes angry:

> "He had felt, at that moment, most acutely in his life, the absence of a father." (P 174 / K 189)

He thinks about all the things he could have had: a warm place to live, land to call his own, all kinds of luxuries in comparison to the hunting cabin. He is jealous of everything Larry has, especially a father's praise: however, his longing for a father blinds him to the fact that Carl seldom praised Larry, and that Larry suffered a lot because of his father. Naturally, Carl knew all along that

Silas was his son – presumably, Larry's mother knows, too – yet there is no question of any of the adults acknowledging this fact. When he is older, Silas understands what kind of father Carl was, realizing that it may have been better to live in the cold cabin for a few years rather than having to deal with a parent like him.

He realizes he was lucky not to have to grow up like Larry did

Perhaps because she never tells him the truth about his father, Silas also has a difficult relationship with his mother. It is only as an adult that he admits to himself that he treated her badly. Initially, he resented the fact that he had to come and live in Mississippi with her, leaving their comfortable home for the bare cabin. She only wants the best for him, encouraging him to study hard and concentrate on his baseball. She even sends him money while he is at school in Oxford so that he does not have to earn his living while studying. He later realizes how much pain he caused her with his infrequent visits, seeming almost embarrassed to be with her. He does not heed her warning that having a relationship with a white girl will end badly, and of course she is proved right. He feels that his lack of understanding about the shame she felt for having to accept the coats was something that formed his character as an adult. Until he was older, he had never considered what the coat symbolized: "defeat, shame, loss, hopelessness" (P 293 / K 305). Without having felt those emotions himself, he had not been able to empathize with Larry, had never thought about what he must have suffered just because he, Silas, had never spoken up. The attack on Larry is the catalyst that finally forces Silas to face up to his past sins and care about other people's feelings. It seems that all of these events will end up making Silas a better person.

He does not appreciate his mother's sacrifices

He has to learn empathy

Carl Ott

INFO AT A GLANCE

He is an abusive father, raising his son by demanding respect instead of showing love

- He dislikes his son, and is scornful both of his appearance and his interests.
- He does not want to teach Larry his trade.
- He enjoys other people's humiliation.
- He takes little responsibility for his past actions.

Larry's father generally comes across as an unpleasant person, with a strong, domineering personality. He is a car mechanic by trade and the owner of the Ottomotive car repair shop. When not at work, he seems to spend most of his time watching television and drinking beer.

Carl has never liked his son

Carl does not have a high opinion of his son. It is clear that he would like Larry to be different in almost every way, something that Larry is very aware of: "He understood that Carl liked most everyone except him." (P 44 / K 61) Physically, Larry reminds his father of the men on Ina's side of the family, who he despises, refusing to have their pictures on the walls. When one of his wife's brothers comes to visit, he arouses Carl's astonishment and scorn by telling them he is a vegetarian, something that Carl considers a "crime against nature" (P 44 / K 62). Furthermore, this uncle had worn his seat belt while being driven to church, which in Carl's opinion is something that only a coward would do. For him, people like Uncle Colin and Larry are "soft and feminine, seat belt users who ate tilapia" (P 45 / K 62).

Tilapia is a kind of fish; Carl believes real men eat meat

As well as disliking his son's physical appearance, Carl disapproves of his hobbies. Although he has taught Larry to shoot and fish, Larry prefers to spend his free time reading. Carl tries to limit the time Larry spends with his head in a book, for example by making him cut the grass at the weekends so that he will have to stay outside, working. Reading makes Larry a "Momma's boy" (P 100 / K 117) in his father's eyes.

Reading is not a proper hobby for a man

Until Larry is twelve, his father refuses to take him along to his repair shop at weekends, saying he is "mechanically disinclined" (P 45 / K 63). Years later, when he is in the army, Larry discovers that he does, in fact, have a talent for being a mechanic; his father had never bothered to pay him enough attention to discover this.

Physical strength is important to Carl

Carl's main problem with Larry is that he is not manly enough. For him, a boy should be able to survive in the wild, to have the awareness of a soldier or a tracker. He tells Larry that he would be an easy target on his own in the wilderness, or if he was forced to go to war: he would be killed because he has no awareness of what is going on around him. Above all, a boy should be able to fight and defend himself with his fists. This is why he forces Larry and Silas to resolve the matter of the borrowed rifle with a fist fight. Carl seems to find it quite exciting, encouraging the two boys to be as violent as they can:

> "From above he heard Carl telling them to bite if they want to, it's allowed, kneeing in the nuts, allowed, kidney punches, rabbit punches, check, check, eye gouging, go ahead, fight dirty […]." (P 102f / K 119)

He enjoys his son's humiliation at the hands of the physically stronger Silas, even joining in by whipping Larry with his belt as he struggles to hit Silas. He must be aware that Silas is also his son, and seems to enjoy playing the two boys off against each other. Many years later, Larry tells Silas that his father had wished he, Silas, was the white boy. Silas is everything Carl would have wished for in a son: tall, good-looking, strong, good at sport, but because he happened to be the wrong color, Carl could never admit their relationship.

Carl's treatment of the two boys is sadistic

As well as disliking his son, Carl does not seem to have much time for his wife. He is polite to her but does not seem to want to spend any time with her beyond eating together. Although he complains about having to go into work on a Saturday, he prefers being at work to staying at home with his family. He clearly does not care that she is humiliated by Alice's presence on their land: when Ina threatens to leave him because of it, he implies that he would be glad of the chance to get rid of her and Larry.

He is an uncaring husband

Likewise, he does not treat Alice well. She had been the family's maid and he had got her pregnant, then sent her away. When she returns to the town with their son, he allows them to live in the old cabin, although the lack of any comfort there does not make this a particularly generous gesture. It seems likely that he has provided the car that Alice gets not long after he stops giving them a ride every morning, but he is not prepared to take further responsibility for them. In fact, before the

He does not do much to help Alice

fight between Silas and Larry, he pretends not to know anything about Silas, demanding to know who his father is, and responds sarcastically to the information that his father is dead: "Well, ain't that sad." (P 101 / K 117) He will never acknowledge that Silas is his son.

He ends up as an alcoholic

Carl has always drunk a lot of alcohol, and starts to drink even more after Larry is accused of killing Cindy. He drinks whiskey rather than beer now, and starts drinking earlier in the day. People avoid his shop, where he had once entertained his friends with stories on a Saturday afternoon, laughing with them and enjoying being the center of attention. He has become a "disheveled drunk sitting in the office smoking cigarettes" (P 155 / K 171). Eventually, he dies after crashing his truck while drunk.

Ina Ott

INFO AT A GLANCE

Larry's mother is devoted to her son

- She is a housewife who is very religious.
- She loves and protects her son, and wants him to be happy.
- Her treatment of Alice is cold and unforgiving.
- She develops dementia after Larry is accused of killing Cindy.

She leads a simple life, taking care of her family

She still remembers her chickens when she has forgotten everything else

Larry's mother is a minor character in the novel, although she appears throughout: in the very first chapter, Larry is going to visit her because she is "having a good day" (P 6 / K 22). This shows that there is something wrong with her, probably an illness of some sort, which will be revealed later in the story. Throughout Larry's childhood and teenage years, Mrs. Ott is a typical housewife. She looks after her husband and son, cooking and cleaning for them. Good manners are important to her. Larry and Carl have to thank her at the end of each meal: "Enjoyed it" (P 82 / K 99), and she does not approve of Carl swearing: "Carl Ott, I said stop it right now." (P 96 / K 112) The hens she keeps in the barn mean a lot to her. She has named them after some of the First Ladies of the United States, and they are one of the last things she can remember clearly when her dementia really takes hold, perhaps because any faint memories she may still have of people are too painful.

Ina is a religious woman who insists that her husband says grace before each meal and volunteers at her local church. Every evening, she goes into Larry's room and prays with him:

> "Please help Larry read good tomorrow, take that stuttering away, and please help his breathing tonight and send him a special friend, Lord, one just for him." (P 97 / K 114)

She understands that her son is lonely and needs a friend, but she does not seem to have any practical solutions to this problem, relying instead on prayer to make everything right: "God's timing [...] is His own." (P 97f / K 114) She has faith that everything will work out in the end for Larry; clearly, however, the friends he does end up making – a black boy and a criminal – are not the sort of people she had in mind.

Her solution to Larry's problems is prayer

When Larry is going to go on a date with Cindy, his mother is very excited for him, much to his embarrassment. He wishes she would stop asking him for details, but she clearly thinks that life is going to be better for him from now on, that he is going to have a girlfriend just like other boys of his age. She gives him a lot of advice on how to treat a girl:

The date with Cindy is a big deal for her, because he has never had any kind of friend before, as far as she knows

> "[...] stand up when she enters a room. Open doors for her. Hold her chair if yall go eat somewhere." (P 138 / K 153)

Larry probably senses that most of this advice will not be needed. His mother does not have any real idea of what it is like to go on a date nowadays, not realizing how much things have changed since she went out with boys, who were expected to behave like a 'gentleman'.

Ina does not really understand what life is like for Larry

Overall, Ina seems to be a kind person. However, her treatment of Silas and his mother show that there is another side to her: her behavior towards them is cold and unforgiving. At first she is surprised when she finds out that Carl and Larry have given Silas and Alice a ride into town. On the following days, she wants more details:

> "Did the woman seem friendly to his father? How did his father act? Was he stiff, the way he could be, was, most of the time? Or was he –" (P 42 / K 59)

She is suspicious of Carl and Alice

Clearly, she suspects that Carl might be continuing his affair with Alice. When Larry tells her that they are living in the old hunting cabin, she makes up her mind to take action. She tells Carl that she will drive Larry to school the next day. When they get to the place on the road where Silas and his mother are waiting, she has Larry wind down the window and passes them two winter coats. She does not even get out of the car to speak to them. It seems that she feels obliged by her sense of Christian duty to make sure that Silas and Alice do not have to go outside in the cold without coats. However, this is not an act of kindness, and she cannot stop herself from making a cutting remark about Alice "using other people's things" (P 43 / K 61). Her sense of duty does not extend to offering them one last ride: she drives off, telling Larry to wind the window up to keep the freezing air out.

She blames Alice for the affair

Carl humiliates his wife by giving Alice a place to live

Ina is humiliated by the continuing presence of Alice and her son on their land, asking Carl how much longer they are going to live in the cabin: "It ain't proper." (P 96 / K 113) It is as if Carl is providing a home for his lover while living with his wife and son. This is one time that Ina attempts to stand up to her husband, threatening to leave him if he does not throw the other two out of the cabin. Carl, however, does not seem particularly upset by this threat; instead, he implies that he would not care if his wife left him. He is in complete control of the situation, whereas his wife seems weak and powerless.

Ina develops dementia when Larry is accused of murder

Cindy Walker's disappearance and the accusations against Larry destroy what family life the Otts had up to that point. They stop talking to each other, and Ina no longer volunteers at her church, knowing she is unwelcome. Gradually, her mental health declines to the point that she can no longer live independently, so Larry puts her in a nursing home. Even there, she is often neglected by the staff, just because of who her son is. Although she still has the occasional day when she can remember Larry and talk about the past, he knows that, effectively, she is just waiting to die.

Alice Jones

INFO AT A GLANCE

Alice loves her son deeply and sacrifices a lot for him

- She takes Silas to live in Mississippi to start a new life.
- She is very attractive to men, many of whom use her.
- She works hard to make a better life for them, which Silas does not appreciate or acknowledge at the time.
- She is afraid of the repercussions of Silas's relationship with Cindy, because she has had a similar experience herself.

Silas's mother has not had an easy life, but does all she can to make the best of things and provide for her son. She had once worked as a maid for the Ott family, but had been forced to leave after Carl Ott made her pregnant. She moved to Chicago, where she and Silas lived a pleasant life in a quiet black neighborhood. It was only when her boyfriend at the time was arrested that she was forced to sell up and decided to move back down south "Cause I got people down there" (P 117 / K 132). However, when Silas asks for more details, she does not tell him anything, and she does not seem to have any family or friends in Mississippi.

As a black woman, Alice's options are limited

Alice is a beautiful woman, and men, both black and white, are easily attracted to her. While she and Silas are traveling south, they encounter various difficulties, and at one point they are stranded late at night with nowhere to stay. Silas realizes that, if there are no other options, his mother would be prepared to sleep with the bus driver who offers them a ride, in order to get a bed for the night. It does not come to that, but it seems that she does allow the driver some kind of sexual favor in return for him driving them to their destination. Alice does not say anything, but she wants to be left alone for a while afterwards: even Silas's presence is too much.

She does what she has to do to survive

Alice does all she can to improve the quality of their lives. She works at two jobs, as well as doing additional cleaning, to save up for a trailer so that she and Silas can move out of the cabin. She is prepared to make sacrifices but insists that Silas has to change his attitude. According to her, he has "had it easier than I ever did" (P 126 / K 142), and he is going to have to stop complaining if they are to make a success of their new life. Silas is aware of everything she has done for him, and, as an adult, feels bad that he did not show her how much he appreciated it at the time. Alice had supported him financially throughout college, and had been hurt that he had wanted to spend so little time with her. With no friends or much contact with other people, she had been "starving from loneliness" (P 178 / K 192). After they moved back to Chabot, she never really laughed again.

Her life has never been easy, but she is prepared to work hard

She leads a very isolated life

Alice has a lot of dignity, and only accepts Carl's and Ina's charity out of necessity. The gift of the winter coats is particularly humiliating for her: she would prefer to freeze rather than take a coat from Mrs. Ott, who blames her for Carl's affair, saying "she'd never minded using other people's things" (P 293 / K 304). However, with no money to buy herself a coat, she has no option but to put it on. Part of the problem is, of course, that she is black, and therefore automatically has a lower status. She has to be polite, laugh at men's jokes, hold her tongue instead of defending herself against injustice. This is why she is upset when she finds out that Silas is dating Cindy and tells him he should break it off, that no good will come of a mixed-race relationship. She is afraid of what will happen to him if he keeps seeing Cindy:

She has to sacrifice her dignity to stay warm

> "Silas, baby, […] you all I got. And you all you got, too. Please tell me you gone stop." (P 233 / K 247)

Silas, however, continues to see Cindy, not listening to his mother's advice. After Cindy's disappearance, Alice persuades the school baseball coach to give Silas a room in his house in Oxford, getting her son away from the situation and sacrificing her one companion in the process. He never lives at home with her again.

Silas does not want to stop seeing Cindy, despite Alice's warning

Cindy Walker

INFO AT A GLANCE

Cindy's date with Larry changes both his and Silas's life forever

- She is pretty and popular.
- She tries to stand up to her step-father, but he becomes gradually more abusive towards her.
- She dreams of escaping their small town with Silas.
- Larry is her victim: she forces him into the situation that leads to his being ostracized by the community.

Cindy Walker lives quite close to the Otts' house, with her mother and step-father. She is a very pretty girl, who can often be seen sunbathing on the porch, or talking to her friends on the phone. As a teenager, Larry often spied on her from the safety of the nearby woods. At school, Cindy is one of the cool kids, who smokes behind the bleachers and has lots of friends. By her own admission, she makes life difficult for her mother with her behavior. However, it is clear that she does not have it easy at home, either. Cecil, her step-father, is clearly attracted to her and acts inappropriately around her, for example by pulling at her towel when she has been in the shower. She often has to deal with this kind of behavior from him:

Larry was attracted to Cindy but would never have dared to admit it

> "He does that kind of shit all the time. […] Trying to see me without my clothes on, come stumbling in the bathroom with his thing in his hand." (P 231 / K 245)

Her step-father abuses her

Cecil also hits her and verbally abuses her, calling her a whore. Although Cindy seems a confident person who is able to give as good as she gets, she is, in fact, trapped in this situation. She cannot go to her mother for help, because she would probably not believe her: "How you tell your momma she married a slime?" (P 231 / K 245)

Cindy's relationship with Silas might be seen as an act of rebellion on the one hand: she knows that Cecil would never allow her to date a black boy, so they have to keep it a secret. On the other hand, she does seem to love him, and since he is a good-looking star of the baseball team, it is easy to see why she is attracted to him.

She wants to run away with Silas

She thinks of Silas as her ticket out of their small town, and is devastated when he refuses to run away with her. Because she is angry with him, she runs away after he drops her back at the road near her house instead of waiting for Larry. This was the last time she was seen alive: it can only be presumed that she went home to find Cecil waiting for her, drunk, who then killed her.

Her argument with Silas ultimately leads to her death

It is easy to feel sorry for Cindy, but she is not a completely sympathetic character. She uses Larry to get out of the house and meet Silas on that fateful night, knowing that she will be able to make him do what she asks. She appeals to his good nature, and possibly he is indeed the only one who could help her. Clearly, she could not know how the evening would end, and that Larry's life would be destroyed because of it. However, she does play with his feelings by allowing him to think that they are going on a real date, and she lies to him about being pregnant to put extra pressure on him, so that he cannot refuse to drive her to her boyfriend. She acts out of desperation, but does not care that she has hurt him in the process. Her excuse may be that she was only fifteen at the time, and not mature enough to consider the consequences of her actions. Certainly she did not deserve to die.

She is able to use Larry because he is too weak to stand up to her

Cecil Walker

INFO AT A GLANCE

Cindy's abusive step-father is presumably also her killer

- Cecil is unemployed and spends his days drinking beer.
- He enjoys playing cruel tricks on Cindy.
- He is abusive towards his step-daughter and clearly wants to have sex with her.
- He allows Larry to take the blame for Cindy's murder.

Cecil grew up in poverty

Cindy's step-father, Cecil, is an unpleasant character. He has had to give up work following an injury, and spends most of his days drinking. With a group of friends, he often goes to Carl Ott's repair shop in the afternoon, to laugh at Carl's stories and drink beer. He is a friend of the Ott family, who Carl has known since his childhood.

Carl reveals that his family were "poor as niggers" (P 141 / K 156), with barely enough clothes to wear. Now, his wife works to provide money for the family.

It is clear that Cecil has a cruel streak. One New Year's Eve, when setting off fireworks with the Ott family, he starts throwing some of them directly at Cindy. The joke is on him when a firework explodes in his back pocket, and everyone present has a good laugh, including Cecil himself. When Larry tells Silas this story, however, he judges Cecil to be "more mean than crazy" (P 91 / K 108), which is perhaps one reason why he tells Cecil to leave Cindy alone later that day.

He enjoys upsetting people

When they start dating, Cindy tells Silas that Cecil is always trying to see her naked. He hits her and threatens to tell her mother that she wants to sleep with him. He has always made her feel uncomfortable, but Cindy had been able to defend herself, talking back to him. The older she gets, however, the more it becomes clear that Cecil wants to have sex with her, and is jealous of her friends. He forces her to come straight home after school and will do anything to stop her from seeing her boyfriend.

He tries to take complete control of Cindy's life

Cindy, desperate to see Silas, persuades Cecil to let Larry take her out on a date. Cecil considers Larry to be a "sissy boy" (P143 / K 159), and threatens him if he dares to even touch her. Despite his aggression, he is sure that Larry would never dare to even kiss Cindy, so he allows her to go out with him. Nobody knows exactly what happened on the night Cindy disappeared, but it seems likely that, after running away from Silas, she went home. Cecil, who was, of course, drunk, must have killed her. Her body is never found. He is aware that he has found an easy scapegoat in Larry. All he has to do is pretend that Cindy did not return home after her date, and the police focus the investigation on the boy, apparently never even questioning Cecil about what he was doing that night. Cecil eventually became very ill and died of cancer, but this cannot make up for the fact that Larry was punished for his crime.

It is easy to convince the police that Larry must be responsible for Cindy's disappearance

Wallace Stringfellow

INFO AT A GLANCE

Fascinated by Larry, Wallace commits a 'copycat murder' in honor of his hero

- From the first time he heard about Larry, Wallace has wanted to meet him.
- He offers Larry friendship, something nobody else has done for years.
- He has several sick fantasies.
- One reason that he kills Tina Rutherford is his certainty that Larry is also a killer.

Wallace wants to be like Larry

Wallace Stringfellow is a young man who befriends Larry. On the face of it, he and Larry have a lot in common: they are both loners in need of some company. However, the more often he comes to visit, the more obvious it becomes that Wallace has developed an unhealthy obsession with Larry and the crimes he believes Larry has committed.

Even as a boy, Wallace is fascinated by Larry

The first time Wallace saw Larry was at church, although he had already heard about him at school. The other kids liked to talk about how Scary Larry had gone to the same school as they did; the teachers warned them to avoid him: "Just let him alone, he might be dangerous. Don't go bothering him." (P 197 / K 211) Wallace, however, was excited by the idea that he might have sat at the same desk as Larry. Thinking back, Larry remembers that particular church service and the skinny boy who kept looking at him, seeming more fascinated by him than afraid of him. Wallace was the main reason Larry never returned to that church. He also realizes that Wallace is the same kid he had once frightened away from his barn by wearing the zombie mask.

Larry accepts Wallace because he is lonely

When he first starts to visit, Wallace seems harmless enough. He volunteers a lot of information about his family and his dogs, and emphasizes the connections between himself and Larry, such as the fact that they both dropped out of high school. Larry is very reserved at first, but after a while gets used to having Wallace around, and misses him when he does not turn up for a few weeks. Although Larry does not like Wallace drinking and smoking weed, he even buys some beer so that he'll have something to offer him. The first Christmas present Larry has received in years comes from Wallace: an old gun, left anonymously on his porch on Christmas Eve. The two of them spend New Year's Eve together, setting off fireworks.

However, after a while it becomes clear that Wallace is a dangerous person. For one thing, he fantasizes about raping women, taking them to the old cabin and attacking them: "They want you to do it." (P 205 / K 219) He also starts trying to make Larry confess to Cindy's murder:

He uses the excuse that women enjoy being mistreated

> "I don't care if you done it or not, took that girl. We'd still be friends if you did." (P 204 / K 218)

Larry's denials make him extremely angry, especially since he has been drinking. He becomes very aggressive, screaming abuse at Larry. It is not long afterwards that he appears on Larry's porch in the middle of the night and confesses: "I done something." (P 268 / K 282) He has been drinking and does not say any more about what he has done. He seems vulnerable: although he somehow felt the need to come out to Larry's place after killing Tina, he does not want to talk about it. When Larry offers him a job as an apprentice, he turns it down, saying he is worthless. It seems that, in a way, he does regret what he has done and does not know what to do next.

Now that he has lived out his fantasy and killed a girl, he seems unsure how he feels about it

A few days later, his next course of action is to put on the zombie mask and shoot Larry. From what he says, it seems that he is punishing Larry for the crime he did not commit. Perhaps Wallace now, more than ever, wants Larry to have killed Cindy, so that, in his head, he can justify his own actions: he was simply copying his 'hero'.

His crime was a form of hero-worship

By the time Silas comes to investigate him, Wallace has clearly reached the point of no return. Realizing that Silas knows the truth about him, he makes a desperate attempt to kill the constable and get away. However, he does not get far and shoots himself before he can be arrested, escaping punishment for all the trouble he has caused.

Themes and Motifs

The ambiguity of belonging

INFO AT A GLANCE

The novel deals with the ambiguity of social identity and personal identity

- Larry is white, but is not accepted by the other white boys.
- He tries to fit in but is not able to connect with his peers because their interests are so different.
- Even after his success at the haunted house, the others reject him.
- As an adult, he has come to terms with his status as an outsider.
- Silas is sure of his identity but finds out that things are not as they seem.
- It is hard for him to accept Larry as his brother – his feelings about it are ambiguous.
- Silas develops a sense of belonging to a place by discovering his roots.

Throughout his life, Larry struggles to be accepted, both by his peers and, later, by society as a whole. On the face of it, it should not be too difficult for him to find his place in society. He is a white boy living in the deep American south, at a time when skin color alone conveyed an automatic sense of privilege. On his first day at middle school in Chabot, a place with a high ratio of black kids and teachers compared to white ones, one of the other white kids says: "Welcome to the jungle" (P 51 / K 69), implying that they are surrounded by wild animals. However, there is no place for Larry among either the white kids or the black ones. The black boys frighten him with their superior physical strength:

Larry is not accepted by the white kids

> "Everything Larry couldn't do – spike a volleyball, throw a football or catch one, fire a dodgeball – these black boys could. Did." (P 40 / K 58)

His interests make him stand out when he wants to fit in

Larry prefers reading, something that none of the other boys can even understand. His lack of interest in sport excludes him.

It would be logical to presume that, with white kids in the minority, Larry would be included in one of their groups. However, the perception that he is weird cancels out the color of his skin: none of the white boys want to be associated too closely with him. The ones that speak to him only do so when their friends are not around. When the boys are in groups, they laugh at Larry "though they'd sometimes let him tag along, the butt of jokes but grateful to be included" (P 52 / K 69). Although he is sometimes allowed to feel that he belongs to the group, he remains an outsider.

Because he is considered strange, nobody wants to risk exclusion from their peer group by getting too friendly with him

Larry really wants to be accepted by the other kids, but does not know how to go about it. For example, he often caught snakes and took them to school, "trying to make people notice him" (P 163 / K 178). Once, on Halloween, he had turned up with a zombie mask. That day, Larry was popular, with lots of kids wanting to see it, even try it on. He is asked to take part in the haunted house event, to give the people at the party a thrill by scaring them. Larry is delighted to be asked, to be part of things for once. Observing him, Silas can see how much he is enjoying himself, and thinks "that tonight Larry must've felt almost normal" (P 164 / K 179). However, once he has finished acting in the haunted house, the other kids make it clear that nothing has changed: he is still a misfit and they do not want anything to do with him. It is easy to imagine how Larry must have felt when he realizes that he still has not done enough to become one of the group:

The zombie mask gives Larry a taste of what it is like to be popular

He realizes he will never be accepted by the other kids

> "[…] Larry stood in the floodlight for a long time. Figuring it out." (P 165 / K 180)

He goes to his car as slowly as possible, giving his schoolmates every opportunity to call him back and invite him to join the party. When the call does not come, he has no choice but to drive home.

After Cindy Walker's disappearance, Larry is ostracized by the local population. There are practically no customers at his repair shop, and the only people who go out to his house are French with the occasional search warrant and drunk teenagers who drive out there to yell insults and vandalize his property. Living in a remote spot anyway, Larry becomes more and more isolated from society, and comes to accept that he will always been an outsider. When he is suspected of Tina Rutherford's abduction, it is clear that his situation would have become

His social isolation continues into adulthood

He cannot imagine ever being completely accepted

worse still if the real criminal had not been found. However, even after it is all over, Larry finds it hard to believe that things will be different for him from now on:

> "He wondered again was it really over. Scary Larry. If anything would really change." (P 308f / K 317)

After all these years, it is almost impossible for him to imagine that he might find a place in society where he would be accepted for who he is, and that his past reputation might be forgotten. At the end of the novel, though, there is hope that he and Silas will manage to renew their friendship. Larry might find a way to belong after all.

Silas is sure of his identity

He is not the person he thought he was

In Silas's case, the ambiguity lies in his family background. Like Larry, on the face of it there does not seem to be any ambiguity about who he is. He is the only son of a black maid, now living in relative poverty in small-town Mississippi. Although he is also a new boy at the middle school, he assimilates quickly and is accepted by his peers, helped by his baseball skills. He has grown up without a father and has come to terms with not knowing who his father was. He is secure in his place in society: he has a responsible job, a loving girlfriend and is a figure of respect in the small town. However, his discovery that Carl Ott was his father, along with the realization that this makes Larry his half-brother, forces him to re-assess his identity. For years, he has resisted Larry's attempts to get back in touch with him, not suspecting the relationship that exists between the two of them. He had always been the cool kid, but now he discovers he has close ties with the social misfit. Silas can imagine that, under different circumstances, they might have been close as brothers, but things did not work out that way:

Silas finds it hard to identify himself as Larry's brother

> "For a moment Silas imagined it had always been like this, that they'd been normal brothers all the years of their rearing, both black or both white, sleeping side by side in matching twin beds. Instead here they were. Strangers. The sons of Carl Ott, injured, bandaged, like survivors of an explosion." (P 289 / K 301)

From the very first time they had met, there had been a connection between them: Silas's interest in reading, Larry's sense that Silas was his "doppelgänger". However, although they are family, the closeness between them has been driven away. On the other hand, there are signs that, having survived the "explosion" of the events surrounding Larry's shooting, they may be able to reconnect after all. In a way, they do belong together, although the relationship between them is not straightforward. Their history will always form the basis for any relationship they have, so there will always be ambiguity there.

The connection that exists between them is ambiguous

The novel also discusses the sense of belonging to a certain place. When Silas and Alice move to Mississippi, he is upset about leaving his nice home, where he had his own room, the pleasant neighborhood, and the city itself:

> "[...] at first, he'd been shocked how quiet the woods seemed compared to Chicago, no crowds, car horns, sirens, no el train clacking by." (P 162 / K 177)

Gradually, however, he became used to the sounds of nature in his new home and got to like them. He also came to appreciate the total darkness of the countryside, where there are no artificial lights. He goes from disliking his new home to feeling as if he belonged there, especially after getting the rifle from Larry and joining the baseball team. This sense of belonging is the reason, in the end, he returned to the area. Silas's mixed feelings about the place are understandable, being torn away from his old life and forced to live a completely different one. However, he belongs there more than he even knew: as it turns out, both of his parents come from there, so he has strong roots in this part of the world. His ambiguous feelings towards the place fade naturally with time.

Silas develops a sense of belonging to the place where his roots are

Friendship and betrayal

INFO AT A GLANCE

More than anything, Larry wants a friend, but the friends he makes cause unforeseen difficulties in his life

- He is not accepted by the other white boys of his age.
- As unlikely as it seems, he and Silas have a lot in common.
- Larry betrays Silas, but Silas's betrayal of his old friend is far more serious.
- It takes Larry a long time to realize that Wallace is not really his friend.

It is unusual for someone like Larry to make friends with a black boy

Every night, Larry's mother prays that God will send him a special friend. His attempts to make friends with his peers at school have failed: to the other white boys in his class, he will always be an outsider, someone to make fun of or to bully. Occasionally, they pretend to be friendly, even inviting him to sit with them at lunch, and he is always "grateful to be included" (P 52 / K 69), but he knows it will not last. When Larry does make a friend, it is someone unexpected: Silas Jones, the new black boy at his school.

Larry first feels a connection between himself and Silas when his father gives Silas and Alice a ride into town. As usual, Larry has got his head in a book, and he sees Silas looking at it, reading the story with him: "Now he [...] saw Silas's lips tense and his eyes moving across Larry's page." (P 40 / K 58) This is the first time Larry has come across someone his own age who is also interested in reading. In the following days, he secretly observes Silas at school:

He feels betrayed because he has felt a real connection to another boy for the first time

> "In the cafeteria Silas sat with a group of black boys, laughing with them, even talking now and again. A betrayal, to Larry. For hadn't Silas been his doppelgänger?" (P 49f / K 67)

On one Sunday afternoon, Larry decides to do something about it. Taking his father's rifle, he goes out to the hunting cabin. After initially thinking that Larry has come to shoot him, Silas gets talking to Larry, eventually persuading him to lend him the rifle, which Larry teaches him to use. Larry feels a lot of sympathy for Silas because he has so little, and instinctively wants to help him, leaving his gloves behind when he goes home in a place where Silas will find them.

This afternoon is the beginning of the friendship between the two boys. As summer goes on, they continue to meet up on the Ott land. Larry is happy because he has someone to talk to about the stories he loves, and to tell about the natural world. Silas also gets a lot out of the friendship. He learns how to shoot and fish, as well as discovering a lot about snakes and other reptiles through Larry's enthusiasm. Even as an adult, he often remembers things Larry taught him that summer. Of course, they cannot tell anyone about their friendship: Larry's parents would never allow it, and Silas reveals that his mother has warned him to stay away from Larry. Larry is sure this must be because he is white: at this point, neither of them know that they are half-brothers.

The summer with Larry left a lasting impression on Silas

Later, when Silas starts playing more baseball, Larry "worried that he was losing him" (P 87 / K 104). In an attempt to keep his only friend, he takes Silas to spy on Cindy Walker, who he has never told Silas about before. Ultimately, this proves to be a bad idea: Carl realizes that Larry and Silas have been spending time together and forces Larry to admit he has lent Silas the rifle. In order to get the rifle back, Carl makes the two boys fight, culminating in Larry calling Silas a 'nigger'. As far as Silas is concerned, this is the end of their friendship:

Silas first encounters Cindy because Larry is trying to impress him

> "[…] Silas looked different than Larry had ever seen him. His eyes now flashed the same fierceness the other black boys at school had […]." (P 103 / K 120)

The use of this racial slur is a betrayal in Silas's eyes, because until that point it had not mattered that he was black and Larry was white. In calling him a nigger, Larry has used the same language as people like Carl or Cecil, with all the implications that come with it: that he is somehow superior to Silas. Larry is sorry as soon as the words are out of his mouth, but he knows that one word has changed everything between him and his friend.

Larry betrays Silas by showing the same racist attitude as other white people

For years afterwards, Silas refuses to speak to Larry, or even acknowledge his existence. Whenever he has to drive past the Ottomotive shop, he stares straight ahead, pretending he has not seen Larry. A few times after Silas's return to Chabot, Larry tries to call him, but Silas

Silas's guilty conscience makes him afraid to meet Larry face to face

never returns his calls. After Larry has been shot, he is annoyed with himself by referring to him as "Larry", indicating that the two of them were closer than he is letting on. He tries to deny this, by saying they simply knew each other at school. Gradually, as the investigation progresses, he admits to Angie that they were more than just schoolmates. However, he resists going to visit Larry at the hospital for as long as he can. It seems that he is still unable to forgive Larry for what he said. He hides the friendship so well that when Larry insists to French while being interviewed in hospital that he and Silas were friends, French does not believe him. Eventually, Silas acknowledges that Larry was his friend, but is unsure whether the opposite is true.

Silas's betrayal was worse because the effects of it were so far-reaching

Ever since their fight, Larry has believed that he was the one who betrayed his and Silas's friendship. He does not know about the secret that has been on Silas's conscience for the last twenty-five years. However, as French puts more pressure on Larry to confess, not just to Tina Rutherford's murder, but also to finally admit that he killed Cindy, Silas finds he cannot remain silent any more. In front of French, he tells the story of what really happened on the night of Cindy's disappearance, revealing that he had been her secret boyfriend and that she had run away from him that night instead of waiting for Larry to pick her up. All this time he has let Larry take the blame, caused him to be ostracized by the community, cost him his business, when he knew that Larry had nothing to do with any of it. When the truth finally comes out, Larry wants nothing more to do with Silas, and even regrets apologizing for calling him a nigger.

Attempts at atonement

Although Silas had kept his distance for so many years, now he cannot do enough for his old friend. He takes care of his chickens, visits his mother in the nursing home and, above all, does all he can to find out who the real killer is and stop Larry from confessing. His investigations lead him to Wallace's house; together with Larry's memory of Wallace's last visit, and his conviction that it was Wallace who shot him, there is enough evidence to show that Wallace must have killed the Rutherford girl. He also cleans Larry's house for him, with

Angie's help, including some surprises such as the installation of satellite TV. He does all he can to atone for his betrayal; however, it is still uncertain whether this will be enough for Larry to forgive him. At the end of the novel, when Larry tells him to bring his Jeep round so that he can take a look at it, we get the impression that a reconciliation between the two men might be possible.

Larry's other main friendship, with Wallace, is based on the loneliness of two misfits rather than anything really personal. As he tells French, he "ain't had a lot of options" (P 286 / K 299) when it comes to making friends. Wallace tells him that they are both alike, two high-school dropouts who find it hard to get along with other people. At first, Wallace is an antidote to Larry's loneliness, and Larry looks forward to his visits, even stocking the refrigerator with beer in the hope that he will keep coming back. He hopes he can help give Wallace a better life by teaching him a trade. He feels sorry for Wallace, who thinks he "ain't worth a shit" (P 269 / K 283), and tries to persuade him that anyone can improve their lives if someone gives them a chance. He thinks he knows why Wallace started to visit him:

Wallace is incapable of returning the friendship Larry offers him

> "I don't think he had anybody to look up to, a daddy or uncle, and crazy as it sounds, he chose me." (P 286 / 299)

However, it soon becomes clear that Wallace is a very different kind of person to Larry, lacking Larry's kindness towards others. In fact, it soon becomes clear that Wallace is fascinated, almost obsessed, by the crimes he thinks Larry has committed, and refuses to believe that he is innocent. Wallace betrays Larry's friendship when he buries Tina Rutherford's body in the old hunting cabin, knowing that suspicion is bound to fall on Larry. The final betrayal is Wallace's attempt to kill Larry, hiding behind the zombie mask so that he does not have to look Larry directly in the eye. In this case, there can be no forgiveness or atonement, as Wallace later kills himself. In a way, Larry feels that it is his fault that Wallace tried to copy him, and that he might have been able to prevent the killing if he had shown more understanding. The boundaries between right and wrong are blurred.

Wallace lacks Larry's kindness and empathy for others

There can be no forgiveness or atonement in this case

The "Crooked Letter": rural Mississippi

INFO AT A GLANCE

The title of the novel refers directly to its setting, showing that it must be significant

- Some things in the novel are not what they seem: there is something "crooked" going on.
- Small-town attitudes make life difficult for Larry.
- Officially, there is no more racial segregation, yet blacks and whites do not mix.
- Even in the present day, there is still evidence of racial discrimination.

The title comes from an aid to spelling for children

In the epigraph, Tom Franklin explains the meaning of the title of the novel: it refers to the way children in the southern US are taught to spell 'Mississippi'. A "crooked letter" is the letter 's'. In his attempts to reconnect with Silas, Larry refers to it: "I just wanted to, you know, say welcome back. To the crooked letter." (P 25 / K 43) Anyone who had grown up in this part of the country would instantly understand what was meant.

The story is not told in a straight line, but is also "crooked"

However, the title does not just stand for the place itself, but can be seen as a symbol. The word "crooked" implies that something is not right, that things are not as straightforward as they seem. Larry's situation illustrates this clearly. The police automatically presume that he is responsible for Tina Rutherford's disappearance; the truth is revealed to be completely different. The way the story is told is not straightforward, either: it jumps between the present day and flashbacks, revealing the whole truth gradually while misleading the reader.

Recurring snake motif

As well as this, the letter 's' calls to mind a snake, a motif that occurs throughout the story. Silas has to kill a snake in a mailbox, while Larry is interested in snakes and often catches them in his barn: it is thanks to him that Silas knows how to deal with the snake in the mailbox. And, of course, Wallace has a whole collection of snakes at his house. Larry takes snakes to school in the hope of attracting attention; instead, it confirms his schoolmates' opinion that he is weird. Wallace's fascination with snakes comes across as far more sinister. His large reptile collection makes his house, and Wallace himself, seem dangerous. Silas instinctively feels uneasy there, and his instinct is proved right when Wallace attacks him.

The setting of the novel plays an important role in the story. In the present, Chabot is a hamlet in decline. Most of the stores and businesses have closed down, forcing its residents to drive to the nearest town for most of their everyday needs. The main employer is the Rutherford timber mill, the only reason why Chabot really continues to exist at all. Even the surrounding areas are changing: a lot of the open woodland where Silas and Larry played as boys now belongs to the mill, and, at some point, most of the trees will be cut down.

There is not much life left in Chabot

With a small town come small town attitudes. Perhaps in a city, Larry would not have been regarded as so strange by his peers: he would not have been the only boy interested in reading rather than sport. Furthermore, in a place like this, everybody knows everybody else, and prejudices are deep-seated. Larry will never shake off his reputation as a misfit, and, because of this, most people are convinced that he must have killed both Cindy Walker and Tina Rutherford, although there is no concrete evidence of either. Larry's social isolation is very much due to the place where he lives.

Narrow-minded attitudes

Since the novel is set in Mississippi, it is unsurprising that race also plays a role in the story. As a black woman growing up in the deep south, Alice has to do as she is told and always show respect to white people. They, on the other hand, can treat her however they like without facing any consequences: Carl Ott sleeps with his maid, and is able to simply send her away when she becomes pregnant. By the time Alice returns to the south with Silas, attitudes are beginning to change, but there is still a marked difference between this part of the country and the north. While waiting at the bus station, the woman in charge of the ticket office tells Silas to come in from the cold, but insists that he speaks to her respectfully:

Silas has to learn to speak differently to white people when he moves south

> "'No,' he said, following her over the cold white tile. 'My mom'll be here in a minute.'
> 'No, *ma'am*,' she corrected. (P 124 / K 140)

The woman immediately guesses that he comes from "up north" (P 125 / K 140) because he does not talk like the local black boys. Black people are not regarded as equals.

In the 1970s and 1980s, black and white people did not really mix in the south

This is why Silas and Larry's friendship is so unusual, even for the 1970s, and why they know their lives will be easier if they keep it a secret. At this time, blacks and whites do not really mix, unless they are forced to do so, for example through the school system. However, this does not result in integration: the black kids stick together, as do the white kids. Cindy too, therefore, makes a daring move by choosing a black boyfriend, and their different races is one reason why Silas breaks it off with her. He cannot realistically see any future for the two of them: "I told her it wasn't gone work" (P 234 / K 247).

Prejudice has not disappeared

In the present day, it is clear that some things have changed. Silas is now the local police constable, with a responsible role in the community: black people have far more opportunities. However, the old attitudes remain to a certain extent. For example, white people still use the now taboo term "nigger", even to people in authority, such as when Brenda in the nursing home responds angrily to Silas's request to clean up Mrs. Ott:

> "Nigger, don't come up in here telling me how to do my job." (P 222 / K 236)

Silas does not respond to the insult itself. Clearly he accepts this attitude as part of the way things are in the south. However, he responds angrily to the situation: he is no longer expected to simply keep his mouth shut. As well as this, the fact that the people he works with, such as French, treat him as an equal, shows that some attitudes, at least, are changing.

How the boy he'd been had grown to be the man he was

INFO AT A GLANCE

Silas has to face up to his past actions and take responsibility for them

- The novel describes how the past affects the present.
- Silas did not speak out about Cindy, through fear of getting into trouble but also because, as a young man, he did not consider the consequences.
- As an adult, he sees how easy it has been to avoid taking responsibility.
- He is forced to find the courage to do the right thing.

As well as being a crime novel, *Crooked Letter, Crooked Letter* is about how the past affects the present. Silas is forced to confront his past and make amends for the trouble he has caused his old friend. The novel shows that the past is never truly over: it may lie hidden for a long time, but a dramatic event, in this case the attack on Larry, can bring everything out into the open again. It is clear that events in their past have made both Silas and Larry the men they are today.

The past has a way of returning

On the face of it, Silas has quite a successful life. He has a responsible job that gives him a certain status in the community; he also has a girlfriend who he loves. However, for twenty-five years he has been carrying the burden of a secret: he is the only person who knows what really happened to Cindy Walker. Keeping this secret cost Larry any chance he might have had of becoming accepted by society.

Silas's secret still affects him today

Why did Silas choose to remain silent? Obviously, things would not have been easy for him if he had admitted the truth: that he, a black boy, was seeing a white girl. As well as this, it was a good time in his life and he did not want to ruin what he had: "You're eighteen and playing ball and everything's going your way." (P 235 / K 248) However, there is more to it than a natural fear of getting into trouble. Angie is incredulous when Silas claims to have simply forgotten about Larry and Cindy, but, at the time, he genuinely did not think about the long-term effects of his actions. It was only much later, when he returned to Chabot, that he "saw the mess I'd made" (P 235 / K 249). As an adult, Silas comes to realize that he

As a young man, it was easy for him to pretend it wasn't his fault

was blind to many things as an adolescent. One incident comes back to him now: the time when Mrs. Ott gave him and his mother winter coats. He himself had simply put the coat on, glad to be warm at last, and was not able to understand why his mother did not immediately do the same. It is only in the light of recent events that he sees how shameful it was for his mother to have to accept the coat from Ina. At the time, he had been oblivious to her feelings:

He was insensitive to his mother's feelings

> "With such gaps in his understanding, he saw very clearly how the boy he'd been had grown to be the man he was." (P 293 / K 305)

Likewise, he had not truly understood what his failure to speak up had done to Larry: how it had destroyed him and his family. It had been easy to use Larry's weirdness as an excuse, to pretend that his feelings did not matter. Silas realizes that he has spent most of his life "[l]etting himself off the hook" (P 273 / K 287); in other words, he has not taken responsibility for his past actions. In the aftermath of Larry's shooting, Silas finally admits to himself that Larry's ostracism was his fault. The next step, he knows, is admitting this to others: to Angie, to the police, and to Larry himself. He wishes there was an easy way to do this, that he could

It is years before he is honest with himself about what happened

> "[…] mow his way back to the boy he'd been and do it differently with Larry, go to the police and say, 'She was with me.'" (P 237 / K 251)

However, nobody is going to make it easy for him now. He recalls what his mother said to him on their journey to Mississippi: "What's missing out of you, Silas?" (P 126 / K 141) Alice feels he has no right to complain about their change in circumstances because she has made sure his life so far has been easier than hers. However, she thinks that he would have become a stronger person if he had had to suffer hardship, as she did: "But now I see what kind of man it's made of you, I don't know if maybe I didn't do you a disservice." (P 126 / K 142) Thinking about it now, Silas realizes that the thing 'missing out of him' is the courage to do the right thing. The time has come to stop being that boy and face up to his past.

Until now, he has lacked the courage to do the right thing

The hardest part for Silas is telling Larry the truth. When he has finally revealed everything he knows, including the fact that they are half-brothers, he is physically exhausted:

Telling the truth is an emotional process

> "Silas felt flattened by the truth, or the telling of it, his lungs empty and raw and the spaces between his eyes throbbing." (P 292 / K 304)

Now that everything is finally out in the open, he can move on and become a different sort of man, one who makes the effort to do the right thing.

The monster behind the mask

INFO AT A GLANCE

The horrifying zombie mask seems to hide a monster

- Larry sees his attacker as a monster in a mask.
- At school, the mask gives him his one taste of popularity.
- As an adult, he uses the mask as a harmless way to scare off an intruder.
- A mask makes the wearer anonymous and distances them from their actions.

Larry's zombie mask appears at different points in the novel. Right at the beginning, he recognizes the mask his attacker is wearing: it is the one he himself bought as a teenager, to his mother's horror and his father's scorn. Lying in a pool of his own blood, he watches the trembling man who has just shot him and feels "a strange forgiveness for him because all monsters were misunderstood" (P 8 / K 24). But does a mask always hide a monster?

Larry is attacked by someone wearing his own zombie mask

Larry loves horror stories, and the realistically gory mask allows him to express this. However, when he takes it to school, at Halloween, the other kids are not disgusted by it. Instead, they are fascinated, gathering round him to get a closer look, some of the cheerleaders, who would normally never have spoken to him, even trying it on. They do not see Larry as a monster at all, but as someone who is cool enough to play an active role at their Halloween party. It is the one time Larry gets a taste of what it is like to be popular: the mask hides the person others usually see. However, when he takes the mask off, he finds nothing has changed: when

The mask allows him to become popular for a day

he stands near his classmates, the mask "deflated under his arm" (P 165 / K 180), he is still the boy that everybody laughs at rather than someone who will be invited to join the party.

He scares Wallace away by wearing the mask

As an adult, Larry does not wear the mask anymore, but he does not throw it away, either. When he realizes that someone has been going into his barn and taking things, he comes up with a plan to make them go away. Taking a day off work, he hides in the barn and when a kid comes in – later revealed to be Wallace – he pulls the mask on and jumps out at the boy, scaring him away. Larry enjoys the incident, and has fun living up to his reputation as "Scary Larry" for once. However, his action is not malicious. He wants to stop the boy from stealing things, and also wants to ensure that he is left in peace from now on, but the action is more a harmless prank than the act of a monster.

A mask can mean anonymity

In trying to get him to confess to rape and murder, French shows Larry that a mask can be used in other ways, to distance yourself from the crime you are committing:

> "[...] you put on the mask so it wasn't you doing it, it was somebody else doing what the women wanted anyway" (P 247 / K 261).

Under the influence of strong painkillers, Larry starts to believe that maybe this is what happened, that he was the monster in the mask who killed the two girls. Luckily, Silas's evidence proves that this was not the case. However, it seems likely that this is what Wallace did to Tina Rutherford. At some point, he stole the zombie mask from Larry's house, and, in his conversations with Larry, he had talked about women "wanting" to be raped. There is evidence that he attacked Tina because he was copying what he believed his hero, Larry, had done. Perhaps this is why Wallace took the mask: he wanted to imagine that Larry was the killer, rather than he himself. Wallace appears to be far more of a monster than Larry ever was.

Wallace can imagine he is Larry when he wears the mask

Structure and Point of View

INFO AT A GLANCE

The story is told through a combination of present-day action and flashbacks

- The novel has nineteen chapters.
- It is told in the present day and through flashbacks.
- The story is told from different points of view.

Crooked Letter, Crooked Letter is a crime novel that is also a story about friendship. It is divided into nineteen chapters and follows events in the lives of the two protagonists, Larry Ott and Silas Jones. The story begins in the present day, when Larry is shot. Chapters two to thirteen alternate between the story of what happens after the shooting, and filling in the background about the events that led up to that incident. The novel contains several flashbacks. Some describe the more recent past, while others take the reader back to Silas and Larry's teenage years. Chapters fourteen to nineteen are set in the present day, and bring the story to its conclusion. In addition to the flashbacks, the story is told using two narrative perspectives: some chapters are told from Larry's point of view, others from Silas's. This allows the reader to get a complete picture of the events described.

The author Tom Franklin describes what it was like, as a white man, to write from Silas's point of view:

> "I have never written from - I'm a white guy - I've never written from the perspective of a black man before, which, you know, was kind of daunting. I don't want to try to appropriate anyone else's voice. It's not first-person I, but it's third-person - you know, he. So I'm not really speaking for Silas, but I'm describing and narrating Silas." (Interview: "Unlikely Friends Color Novel's Deep South", http://www.npr.org/templates/story/story.php?storyId=130303007)

Seeing things from the perspective of both protagonists allows the reader to identify with the characters and understand what motivated them to act in certain ways. It also adds to the suspense, allowing the whole story to be gradually revealed, first from Larry's point of view and then from Silas's.

About the Author

Tom Franklin was born in 1963, in a small town in Alabama with a population of about five hundred people. He studied English at the University of South Alabama, doing various manual jobs to support himself while getting his B.A. He then studied for a Master of Fine Arts at the University of Arkansas, where he met his future wife, the poet Beth Ann Fennelly. As well as writing, he teaches at the University of Mississippi.

Crooked Letter, Crooked Letter (2010) is his best-known novel, which won the Crime Writers' Association Gold Dagger Award. However, he is not purely a crime writer: in fact, he is often described as a "southern writer", as his novels are set in the American South and paint a vivid picture of life in that part of the world, including themes such as racism and the decline of small-town life.

There are some parallels between him and the characters in *Crooked Letter, Crooked Letter*. He grew up in a similar place to Chabot and also spent his free time as a child roaming the woods. Like Larry, his father was a mechanic. He himself loved horror stories, especially by Stephen King. His painful descriptions of high school also reflect some personal experience.

❸ Fast Facts

Outline 1: Timeline and Narrative Perspective

Outline 2: Silas and Larry – Key Moments

Outline 3: The Ambiguity of Belonging

Outline 4: The "Crooked Letter"

Outline 5: Betrayal

Outline 6: Friendships

Outline 7: Recurring Motifs

Outline 1: Timeline and Narrative Perspective

Chapter	Time / Point of view	Main events
One	present (Larry)	Larry is shot by an intruder wearing his zombie mask and left to die on the floor in his house.
Two	present (Silas)	Silas finds M&M's body; he sends the ambulance to Larry's house.
Three	flashback (Larry)	Larry and Silas first meet; Larry is tricked into insulting a black girl at school; Larry befriends Silas and teaches him to shoot.
Four	present (Silas)	Silas and French investigate the crime scene at Larry's house; Silas discovers a message from Larry on his answering machine.
Five	flashback (Larry)	Larry takes Silas to spy on Cindy; Silas defends Cindy against Cecil; Carl forces the boys to fight.
Six	present/flash-back (Silas)	Silas finds the photo of his mother in Larry's attic; he remembers his journey from Chicago to Mississippi with his mother.
Seven	flashback to 1982 (Larry)	Larry's date with Cindy; she persuades him to drive her to her boyfriend's place and is never seen again.
Eight	present (Silas)	Silas and Angie talk about the case; he tells her about Larry's zombie mask; Silas visits Larry and Mrs. Ott for the first time; he encounters Wallace driving his four-wheeler; he discovers a grave in the old hunting cabin.
Nine	flashback (Larry)	Wallace starts visiting Larry; Larry realizes he had seen him as a boy; Wallace turns on Larry when he won't admit to killing Cindy.
Ten	present/flash-back (Silas)	It is confirmed that Tina Rutherford's body was in the cabin; Larry is now the only suspect; Silas guards his hospital room at night and tells Larry not to confess; he discovers Mrs. Ott is being neglected in the nursing home; he tells Angie about his relationship with Cindy; they realize Cecil must have killed her.

Eleven	present (Larry)	Larry regains consciousness; French interviews him and tries to get a confession.
Twelve	present (Silas)	Silas rushes to the hospital when he hears Larry is awake; Larry is glad to see him until he admits what really happened on the night Cindy disappeared; Silas goes to a bar to get drunk and meets Irina again; she tells him about her roommate who narrowly avoided being raped by Wallace.
Thirteen	present (Larry)	Larry is still restrained on his hospital bed; he remembers that Wallace almost confessed some-thing to him a few nights before the shooting; Larry realizes the truth and asks to talk to French.
Fourteen	present (Silas)	Silas goes to Wallace's house; Wallace sets his dog on Silas and shoots him.
Fifteen	present (Larry)	Larry hears that Silas has been shot; he tells French about Wallace; Silas is put in the same room as Larry after his surgery.
Sixteen	present (Silas)	Silas tells Larry they are half- brothers; Larry asks to be moved to another room.
Seventeen	present (Larry)	Silas has lots of visitors; it is confirmed that Wallace killed Tina; Silas is discharged from hospital.
Eighteen	present (Silas)	Silas visits Larry but Larry will not speak to him; he and Angie clean up Larry's house.
Nineteen	present (Larry and Silas)	Larry walks out of the hospital; Silas finds him and drives him home; Larry offers to repair the Jeep.

Outline 2: Silas and Larry – Key Moments

Larry and Silas meet for the first time.	• Silas shows interest in Larry's book. • Larry senses that Silas is his "doppelgänger".
Larry initiates the friendship.	• He teaches Silas to shoot and fish. • He lends Silas the rifle.
Silas only visits Larry at home once.	• They catch snakes in the barn. • Silas cuts the grass and Carl praises Larry for Silas's work.
Larry and Silas secretly watch Cindy and her father.	• Silas jumps to Cindy's defense. • Carl makes the boys fight for the rifle. • Larry insults Silas and their friendship ends.
Larry drives Cindy to meet her boyfriend, not knowing it is Silas.	• She does not turn up at the agreed meeting place. • Larry is blamed for her disappearance because Silas does not speak out.
Larry tries to get back in contact with Silas after he returns to Chabot.	• Silas ignores his calls and pretends he does not have time for his old friend.
Silas saves Larry's life by sending the ambulance to his house.	• Silas discovers he and Larry are half-brothers. • He reveals what really happened the night Cindy disappeared.
Larry is angry with Silas and wants nothing to do with him.	• Silas tries to make amends by visiting Larry in hospital and cleaning up his house. • He finds Larry walking home and drives him there. • Larry offers to fix the Jeep.

Outline 3: The Ambiguity of Belonging

Belonging

- being certain of one's place in society or of one's personal identity

Ambiguity

- social or personal identity is not always as clear-cut as it seems

Larry: ambiguity of social identity

- The black kids and white kids form two distinct groups → they do not mix.
- Larry is white, but is not accepted by the other white boys.
- He has different interests → the other boys laugh at him.
- He longs to be accepted but does not know how → his attempts to attract their attention, e.g. by bringing snakes to school confirm his reputation as 'weird'.
- Wearing his zombie mask at the haunted house → the one time he thinks he has been accepted.
- It is an illusion → his peers still want nothing to do with him.
- As an adult it seems he will always be "Scary Larry" → even after his name has been cleared, he wonders if he will ever lose his reputation as an outsider.

Silas: ambiguity of personal identity

- His identity seems clear.
- He finds it easy to integrate at his new school → fits in with the other black kids.
- He grew up not knowing his father → and has come to accept that.
- The discovery that Carl Ott is his father makes him question his identity → he is not the person he thought he was.
- The fact that he and Larry are half-brothers forces him to reassess their relationship → one reason why he tries to make amends for his behavior.
- Silas was the cool kid but proves to have a close connection with the misfit → ambiguity.
- His sense of belonging to Mississippi → mixed feelings at first, but his roots are there.

Outline 4: The "Crooked Letter"

- An 's' looks like a snake.
- Snakes play an important role in the novel, e.g. the snake in the mailbox; Larry likes catching them; Wallace keeps snakes.

- The storyline is 'crooked'.
- The story is not told chronologically, but by means of flashbacks.
- Things are not what they seem: the truth is revealed gradually.

- A "crooked letter" is the letter 's'.

The "Crooked Letter" symbolizes Mississippi itself.

The title of the novel refers to the way children in the American south are taught to spell "Mississippi".

- Something in the small town is 'crooked', i.e. is not right.
- Everyone believes in Larry's guilt, but they are looking at things the wrong way.

- The setting implies certain attitudes that are often found in the rural south: racism and discrimination, unwillingness to accept people who do not fit in.

- In a small place, everybody knows each other's business.
- There is no escape for Larry: people will always see him as a killer.
- He has been ostracized for twenty-five years.

- Larry's and Silas's friendship is unusual.
- People would disapprove if they knew a white boy was friends with a black boy.
- Silas's relationship with Cindy is dangerous for the same reason.
- His mother has had experience of this and tries to warn him off.

Outline 5: Betrayal

- Larry calls Silas a 'nigger' in the heat of the moment: he feels shame because he is being defeated in the fight in front of his father.
- He instantly regrets saying it, but it destroys their friendship.

- Silas does not confess that he was with Cindy the night she disappeared.
- Larry took the blame and was ostracized from that day on.
- He lost his business and lived in isolation.
- Silas allowed Larry to suffer for years.

Several of the characters betray each other in the novel. They betray trust, keep secrets or reveal them, sometimes with disastrous consequences.

- Silas betrays Cindy: he breaks up with her to save his baseball career.
- She thought he would save her from her family situation.
- He lets her run off in the dark without checking to see if she is all right.
- If he had spoken up, her killer might have been found.

- Cindy betrays Larry: she lets him think she really wants to go on a date with him.
- She uses him because she knows he will not refuse to help her.

- Carl Ott betrays his wife by sleeping with their maid.
- He brings shame on Ina by allowing Alice and Silas to live on their land.

- Larry has "betrayed a trust between himself and his father" (P 43 / K 60) by telling his mother about giving Alice and Silas a ride.
- His mother gives the two of them coats, but makes it clear that there should be no future contact.

- Wallace betrays Larry's friendship.
- Larry thinks he has found a new friend at last.
- Wallace is only interested in the crimes he thinks Larry has committed.
- He kills Tina Rutherford to be like his 'hero'.
- He tries to destroy Larry too by shooting him.

Outline 6: Friendships

Larry and Silas

- Unlikely friendship between a black boy and a white boy → also between a popular, 'cool' kid and a social misfit
- Disapproval of their parents → Carl does not mix with black people; Alice wants Silas to stay away from the Ott family because of how they treated her.
- They feel a connection → a shared interest in stories.
- They enjoy each other's company in the woods: shooting and fishing.
- Larry teaches Silas about the natural world.
- Their friendship ends when Silas thinks Larry is racist like all the other white people.
- They are half-brothers → there is still a connection between them.
- Because of this, they are able to rekindle their friendship.

Larry and Wallace

- Two outsiders are drawn together.
- Larry does not have any other social contacts.
- Wallace looks up to him → Larry is a father figure in some ways.
- What Larry initially sees as friendship is really an unhealthy obsession with his 'crimes'.
- Larry is wrong to trust Wallace → it nearly costs him his life.

Silas and Cindy

- She is first attracted to him when he stands up for her against her step-father.
- He notices her watching him at baseball practice.
- They have to keep their relationship secret.
- They are in love → Cindy sees Silas as her ticket out of Chabot.
- Silas does not see a future for them because of their different races.
- He would have to sacrifice too much to be with her.

Outline 7: Recurring Motifs

Snakes

- Symbol of danger
- There is a snake in Irina's mailbox.
- Larry brings snakes to school → wants to impress the other kids.
- Larry and Silas catch snakes in the barn → Silas learns a lot from Larry.
- Wallace keeps lots of snakes at his house → he sent the snake to Irina's roommate.
- A snake is found next to Silas's body after Wallace has shot him.

Guns

- Larry is found shot, with a gun in his hand, although he is not allowed to own one.
- As a constable, Silas has a gun but has never used it.
- Carl has a number of firearms → normal in that part of the country.
- Larry lends Silas a rifle and teaches him how to use it.
- Carl makes the two boys fight for the ownership of the gun.
- Larry receives an anonymous Christmas present → Wallace wants him to be able to protect him-self → he ends up shooting Larry with it.

Books

- Larry always has his head in a book → this makes him a 'Momma's boy' in Carl's eyes.
- He first connects with Silas when he realizes Silas is interested in his book.
- His house is overflowing with books.
- Since he has no customers, he spends his days reading.
- Books have always been a form of escape for Larry.

4 Model Questions and Answers

1. The Title of the Novel
2. Larry and Silas as Boys and as Men
3. Silas's Responsibility for his Past Actions
4. The Father-Son Relationships in the Novel
5. Larry and Wallace
6. The Zombie Mask
7. The Ambiguity of Belonging

1. The Title of the Novel

What is the significance of the title of the novel? What role does the novel's setting play?

Crooked Letter, Crooked Letter is part of a phrase taught to southern school children, to help them remember how to spell 'Mississippi'. The "crooked letter" is the letter 's'. Anyone who had grown up in that part of the country would immediately understand that the novel was set in Mississippi. However, the title can also be seen as a symbol for certain aspects of the story.

- 'Crooked' is the opposite of 'straight': this could be applied to the way the story is told. Instead of telling the story from beginning to end, the novel switches between the present and the past, filling in important details by means of flashbacks. This adds suspense, an important feature of any crime novel. The reader is not given all the facts right from the start; instead, it is gradually revealed that things are not quite as straightforward as they seem. The more we discover about the protagonists' backgrounds, the better we understand what motivates them to act as they do.
- The word 'crooked' can also imply something wrong, something dishonest, which certainly applies to this story. Larry has been blamed for the disappearance of Cindy Walker, and, when another girl goes missing, he instantly becomes the main suspect. However, as the novel progresses, we find out that this general view of Larry is wrong, and that he in fact had nothing to do with killing the girls. No real effort is made to find out what really happened until it is nearly too late.
- When Larry tries to get back in touch with Silas, he does not welcome him back to Chabot, but to "the crooked letter" (P 25 / K 43), showing that this phrase symbolizes the place itself. The setting plays an important role in the novel. First of all, there are the typical attitudes of people living in a remote rural part of the American south. They are suspicious of anyone who does not conform, which is why Larry, with his love of reading and interest in snakes, is dismissed as an outsider.
- The police do not seem to look very hard for other suspects in the cases of the missing girls: Larry's reputation as a misfit and the fact that he had actually been with Cindy the night she disappeared seem to be enough proof of his guilt. Ever since that night, he has remained "a person of interest" (P 6 / K 22) as far as the police are concerned. Because it is such a small place, everybody knows about Larry: he will never be able to shake off his reputation as a loner who probably enjoys killing women.
- Race also plays a role in this part of the world: blacks and whites do not really mix, although the children are forced to: "[...] Larry wondered why

grown-ups made the kids mingle when they themselves didn't." (P 51 / K 69) This naturally leads to tensions among the children, and Larry in particular suffers, accepted neither by the black kids nor the white ones. This is why making friends with Silas is "an interesting idea" (ibid.), and something that the two of them have to keep secret. Likewise, Silas's and Cindy's relationship goes against the norms of small-town Mississippi, and their different races is one reason why Silas breaks things off. In the end, he heeds his mother's warning, spoken from bitter experience, that "nothing good ever come out of colors mixing" (P 232 / K 246). Because she is so upset that Silas does not want to be with her anymore, Cindy runs away from him, presumably to be killed by Cecil later that evening. Indirectly, therefore, it is the tensions between blacks and whites in this Mississippi town that lead to her murder and start off the chain of events that ends with the shooting of Larry Ott.

2. Larry and Silas as Boys and as Men

Compare Silas and Larry as boys and as men. How did their childhood influence the men they became?

On the face of it, Silas and Larry could not have been more different as boys. Silas is sporty, a star baseball player, and popular with the other kids. Larry, on the other hand, is an outsider, mainly interested in reading, and bullied by both the black kids and the white ones. Moreover, since Silas is black and Larry is white, a friendship between the two of them is risky in 1970s Mississippi.

However, there are, in fact, several similarities that draw the boys to each other. Larry sees that Silas is also interested in books: Silas enjoys listening to Larry's favorite horror stories. And, although he is not good at sport, Larry does enjoy outdoor activities such as shooting and fishing, and knows a lot about nature. Silas likes spending time outside with him and learns a lot.

As a teenager, Silas is a lot braver than Larry. When the two boys see Cecil mistreating Cindy, it is Silas who leaps to her defense: "Yall leave that girl alone" (P 93 / K 110). Cecil and Carl are shocked that a black boy would dare to challenge them; Larry, on the other hand, remains hidden. He later tells Silas that he wanted to help, but they both know he does not have the courage. Likewise, Larry is afraid to stand up to his father and so cannot avoid the fight with Silas. When, desperate to be released from Silas's grasp, Larry blurts out a racial slur, Silas is convinced that Larry is just like the other white people, considering himself superior to blacks. It almost seems as if their friendship has been a lie, and Silas cuts off all contact with Larry from that point onwards.

However, as men, Silas is the one who lacks courage: it is what is 'missing out of him'. It is very difficult for him to admit his part in Cindy's disappearance, even though doing so will clear Larry's name. After Larry is shot, he often reflects on his childhood and wonders how he might have done things differently. In particular, the evening of the haunted house party stands out in his mind. He wonders how their lives might have turned out if he made sure Larry was included, instead of shutting him out: "What if he'd just reached out and took Larry's shoulder, said, 'Wait'?" (P 290 / K 302) Perhaps Larry would have grown up to be a different person, one who could not be so easily manipulated.

For Larry, Silas's revelations are a turning point. Up until then he has accepted the way people treated him after Cindy's disappearance, unable to change their belief that he is a killer. He has always remained polite and humble, keeping himself to himself, feeling safer in the isolation of his home. Now, however, he sees why his enforced isolation has allowed people to blame him for Tina Rutherford's death, too, and why he has allowed them to do so: "[...] maybe he'd been shoved away from everybody for so long all he was was a sponge for the wrongs other people did. Maybe, after all this time, he'd started to believe their version of him." (P 270 / K 283f) Finding out that he has suffered needlessly for twenty-five years makes him see things in a different light: he is determined not to be a victim any more. He stops protecting Wallace and tells French what he knows. He also stops talking to Silas, not seeing why he should simply forgive him.

Both men suffer greatly in the aftermath of Larry's shooting, both physically and mentally, yet both recover to become stronger versions of themselves. Silas realizes that the world of adulthood is just as "full of unknowns" (P 305 / K 314) as the world of childhood was, yet he sees things positively now: there is "some future still ahead" (ibid.), especially if they can recapture some of the world of their boyhood.

3. Silas's Responsibility for his Past Actions

"Letting himself off the hook had been his way of life." (P 273 / K 287) In what ways has Silas let himself off the hook? How does he take responsibility for his past actions?

For many years, Silas has had a guilty secret. He was Cindy Walker's boyfriend, and was with her on the evening she was seen for the last time. He knew she had asked Larry to drive her to his place, and to meet her again later and then drive her home, as if they had been together the whole time. This was the only way for Silas and Cindy to meet, as at that point in time Cecil was becoming more and more possessive of his step-daughter. He only let her go out with someone who would never dare to do anything to her, in other words, Larry. Larry keeps his side of the bargain and pretends he was with Cindy; as a result, he is blamed for her disappearance.

Silas knows that Cindy had run back to her house before Larry even turned up, and therefore he could not have had anything to do with her disappearance. However, he chooses to keep this information to himself. One reason for this was obviously to avoid getting into trouble himself. The consequences for admitting he had been seeing Cindy would have been serious: perhaps this was one way for Silas to justify keeping his silence. Another reason is that, as an eighteen-year-old, he did not really consider how his actions would affect Larry: "Things ain't so clear when they're happening." (P 235 / K 248) At the time, it was his mother who solved the immediate problem for him: she arranged for him to change schools, to move to another town and live in his baseball coach's basement. This allowed him to put the events in Chabot behind him: "I was glad to go. It was a whole lot better up there. Better field, school." (P 234 / K 248) It was easy for him to pretend to himself that he had to go away because of his promising baseball career, that his move north had nothing to do with Cindy.

Even when Larry is in hospital after the shooting, Silas still seems to hope he will not have to tell the whole truth: he tells Angie he thinks it would be better for Larry if he never recovered from his injuries. She sees at once what he means: "Better for you?" (P 235 / K 249), and he has to admit that yes, it would be easier for him, too. If Larry died now, Silas would be 'off the hook' forever: the police would continue to believe in Larry's guilt and the case would be closed.

However, in the end Silas realizes that taking responsibility for his past actions is the right thing to do. Angie is the first person he tells what really happened that night. Then, knowing that French is close to making Larry confess to killing both Cindy and Tina Rutherford, he rushes to the hospital room and reveals the truth at Larry's bedside. It is not easy for him to do so, but he knows he has to. Larry has always been loyal: "We were friends. Weren't we, Silas?" (P 254 / K 268), but Silas knows he has betrayed that friendship, and it is now time to make things right.

Larry has been punished for twenty-five years for something he did not do. Now, it is Silas's turn to suffer. After his confession, Larry wants nothing to do with him, even after finding out that they are half-brothers. Silas tries to make amends through his actions: he feeds the chickens, goes to visit Larry's mother, cleans his house for him. He comes to visit every day, even though Larry does not want to see him. He knows that all of these things are "penance" (P 303 / K 313) for his past sins, and it is hard to say whether he will receive Larry's forgiveness. At the end of the novel, it seems that they will be able to renew their friendship after all.

4. The Father-Son Relationships in the Novel

"He wished you'd been the white one." (P 293 / K 304) Analyze the father-son relationships in the novel.

Larry has a difficult relationship with his father. Carl Ott has never made a secret of the fact that he would prefer a different type of son: one who was tall and handsome, good with his hands, interested in more than reading horror stories. Because his wife takes his son's side, Carl sees him as a "Momma's boy" (P 100 / K 117) who has always got his head in the clouds. A son of his should be good at fighting, and he finds it pathetic that "when it comes to knuckles, you can't even get your own daddy's gun back from the boy that stole it" (ibid).

Larry tries to win his father's approval, for example by going to work with him in the car repair shop on a Saturday. Even there, though, he keeps out of his father's way, afraid of making him angry. He is scared to admit that he lent the rifle to Silas, and is too nervous to ask to borrow the car for his date with Cindy, getting his mother to pave the way for him. The only time his father seems pleased with him is when he hears about the date. Carl jokes around with Larry about the kind of movie they are going to see, and even gives him twenty dollars for the evening, something that makes Larry almost speechless with astonishment. At the meal they share before Larry goes to meet Cindy, his father tells one of his funny stories and the whole family laughs together. It is to be the last time they ever come close to being a happy family.

Although it is not stated specifically in the novel, it is obvious that Carl knows Silas is also his son. He has a cruel sense of humor, and clearly takes great pleasure in playing the two boys off against each other when he forces them to fight: "Peers we got us a dispute between the races, here." (P 101 / K 117) He orders Silas to tell him who his father is, and reacts with heavy sarcasm when Silas says he is dead, enjoying the secret knowledge that Silas is his son. He does his best to provoke the two of them into fighting: "Now Larry here's a little older, but on the girly side, so I figure it's even." (P 102 / K 118) He seems to enjoy watching Larry get a beating, and to be glad that Silas has won: "Looks like you won yourself a rifle, boy" (P 103 / 119). Physically, Silas is everything Carl would have wished for in a son, except that his skin is the wrong color. Much later, Larry confirms this: "He wished you'd been the white one" (P 293 / K 304).

On some level, Larry knew from the first time they met that Silas was his brother. He senses his father's preference for the son he cannot acknowledge. When Carl praises Larry for cutting the grass, although it was Silas who did the work, Silas sees the other boy "looking over to where [he] had run, staring, it seemed, directly at him" (P 174 / K 189). Larry's jealousy can be felt here: finally he has got the praise he always wanted from his father, yet it applies to another boy. Larry knows he will never gain his father's approval, no matter how hard he tries.

Silas has grown up without a father, and tells Larry "[i]t wasn't easy without one" (P 293 / K 305). Ironically, he had been envious of Larry, wishing he had a warm house with a big barn and acres of land to call his own. He had never had a father figure in his life: his mother's boyfriend in Chicago would have preferred it if Silas had not existed, and Alice had not had a partner since moving south. He would have been glad of a father, even one like Carl. Larry takes away any illusion he may have had about this: "You think it was better [...] living with him?" (Ibid.) Silas has to admit that it probably was not. He and Larry had shared the same father, and yet neither of them had experienced a positive father-son relationship.

5. Larry and Wallace

Larry says of Wallace "I thought he was my friend" (P 286 / K 299). Why did he think so? Were they really friends?

When Wallace Stringfellow starts driving over to Larry's place, he is the first proper visitor Larry has had in years. Since his mother moved into the nursing home, Larry has lived alone. What's more, his house is in an isolated spot, which means that nobody comes past unless they have a reason to do so. Larry has got out of the habit of dealing with other people, and in many ways his life is easier without social contacts.

On his first visit, Wallace pretends that he works for a satellite TV company and has come to sell Larry a dish. Larry tells him he does not want one, but, instead of leaving, Wallace sits down and makes himself comfortable. Larry does not talk much, or give Wallace any information about himself. This does not seem to matter to Wallace, however, who talks a lot about himself and also asks Larry a lot of questions. Larry answers him politely, but is very reserved, being unused to social interactions. However, as Wallace's visits become more frequent, Larry gets used to having him around and even misses him during his absences.

Wallace emphasizes that he and Larry are alike: "Couple a dropouts ain't we." (P 187 / K 201) On the face of it, there are similarities between the two men: they are both social misfits who were bullied at school, they do not really have any work and they live in isolation. However, they are clearly very different types of people. Wallace talks all the time, drinks heavily and smokes weed, whereas Larry is quiet, does not even have any alcohol in the house and refuses Wallace's offer of a joint. Because Wallace is his only social contact, he does seem like a friend to Larry. In other ways, Larry almost feels like a father to the younger man, and imagines saving him from himself: "[...] he'd offer him a job on the condition the boy stop drinking and smoking so much" (P 208 / K 222). He later tells French that Wallace seemed almost to look up to him, as the father he had never had. However, this is not really friendship, and, of course, his relationship with Wallace takes a sinister turn.

Although Wallace is very friendly at first and almost protective of Larry, offering to get him a dog and secretly giving him a gun for Christmas, it soon becomes clear that he has an unhealthy obsession with the older man. He believes that Larry is guilty of killing Cindy Walker, and tries to make him admit it, saying that he would not report Larry to the police: "We friends, and a friend, a best friend, he wouldn't never do you that way, wouldn't never call the law on his friend, no matter what his friend done." (P 205 / K 219) When Larry insists that he has never hurt anyone, Wallace turns violent, screaming abuse at him and smashing the windshield of his van. Wallace had believed that Larry was his friend because he thought they shared the desire to hurt women: it makes him furious to think that this might not be true after all. Later, after Larry realizes Wallace was the one who shot him, he sees that there was no real friendship involved. However, he still feels responsible for the younger man and wonders whether, if he had talked to Wallace instead of sending him away, he could have prevented Tina Rutherford's death.

6. The Zombie Mask

Why does Larry feel sorry for his attacker? What does the zombie mask represent in the novel?

Lying on the floor, bleeding heavily, Larry looks at the man in the zombie mask and feels "a strange forgiveness for him because all monsters were misunderstood" (P 8 / K 24). He feels sorry for the man because he understands what it is like to be considered a 'monster'. For many years, the local people have believed he himself is a monster who murdered a young girl, yet he knows that this is not true.

- Larry's zombie mask is mentioned several times in the story. On the one hand, it represents horror: Larry loves horror stories, so it is natural that he would like a mask like that. It symbolizes the horror of his shooting, of someone waiting at his house and trying to kill him. He himself uses it to scare the young Wallace away from his barn, enjoying the fright that the boy gets. However, he also wants to prevent Wallace from hurting himself by making sure he does not come back, so his intentions are actually good.
- When Larry wears takes the mask to school at Halloween, it gives him a taste of popularity. The other kids love it, and, for once, see him as cool rather than weird. It allows him to feel "almost normal" (P 164 / K 179). However, the mask does not, after all, mean that he is accepted. After the party, his peers still want nothing to do with him, and simply ignore him. The mask cannot hide the person he really is: he is still a misfit.
- The mask also represents anonymity, creating a physical barrier between a crime and the person committing it: "[...] you put on the mask so it wasn't you doing it" (P 247 / K 261). Wallace clearly admires Larry for the crimes he is supposed to have committed: in a twisted sense, Larry is his hero. This is why he steals the mask and wears it when he shoots Larry – and probably when he killed Tina Rutherford – he is not Wallace Stringfellow then, but "Scary Larry". In Wallace's case, however, the mask cannot hide his true nature: he really is a monster.

7. The Ambiguity of Belonging

What is meant by "the ambiguity of belonging" and how does the term apply to the novel?

The concept of 'belonging' can be used in a variety of contexts.

- It can refer to belonging to a particular social or ethnic group, a particular class, or a place.
- It can also refer to a person's sense of personal identity, or belonging to a family or other group.

However, a person's sense of belonging might not be as clear-cut as it seems at first glance. This is where the idea of belonging can become ambiguous: the concept is open to interpretation.

It would be natural to think that Larry, as a white boy, would be able to hang out with the other white boys at his school. However, because he is seen as a strange person with unusual hobbies, he is not accepted by his white peers. He obviously cannot join the black kids, either, so he is stuck somewhere in the middle of these two groups, laughed at by both. He is happy on the occasions when the white boys "let him tag along" (P 52 / K 69), because then he feels less exposed, more part of a group and, for a short while, protected from the kids who are aggressive to him. This sense of belonging is only an illusion, though. For example, when he is encouraged by two boys in his class to shout "Monkey Lips" (P 55 / K 73) at one of the black girls, none of the other white kids defend him when he gets into trouble. In fact, when the black kids start throwing their books at Larry, they join in the laughter at his expense. It is made quite clear to Larry that he is not accepted, and probably never will be.

Silas was secure in his identity until, by chance, he comes across a photo that shows him he is not the person he thought he was. It shows his mother holding Larry as a baby, and he realizes she must have been the Ott's maid. He puts two and two together and sees the whole truth: Carl Ott is his father, who sent Alice away when she got pregnant. The knowledge that Larry is his half-brother changes his perception on things. As boys, he and Larry had had a special connection, which had been destroyed by Larry's insult. Since then, Silas has ignored his old friend, but he cannot do so any more. Discovering their relationship gives him a moral obligation to finally tell the truth about him and Cindy, to stop an innocent man from being further punished. After all they have been through, they cannot be "normal brothers" (P 289 / K 301), but they do somehow belong together, which is perhaps why, in the end, they are able to start repairing their relationship.

There is also the theme of belonging to a place. When Silas first moves to Mississippi, he feels like an outsider, missing the sounds and sights of the big city. However, after a while he assimilates, learning to shoot and playing a lot of baseball: "[…] I felt like I belonged here. It's part of why I came back" (P 163 / K 178). And, in fact, he does belong there: it is where both his parents come from, so his roots are there. He is not a city boy, as he had once thought; instead, the rural south is part of his identity.

Further Reading

Tom Franklin, *Poachers*, New York 1999 (short story collection).
Tom Franklin, *Hell at the Breech*, New York 2003.
Tom Franklin, *Smonk*, New York 2006.
Tom Franklin / Beth Ann Fennelly, *The Tilted World*, New York 2013.

Useful links

Reviews of *Crooked Letter, Crooked Letter* and interviews with Tom Franklin:

http://www.npr.org/templates/story/story.php?storyId=130303007
("Unlikely Friends Color Novel's Deep South")
http://www.patheos.com/blogs/karenspearszacharias/2011/01/17/interview-with-author-tom-franklin/
http://bookgroup.info/041205/interview.php?id=80
http://bookfinds.com/blog/2010/10/20/crooked-letter-crooked-letter-by-tom-franklin-interview/
https://www.youtube.com/watch?v=4VCaiPHtHOQ
("Video interview about *Crooked Letter, Crooked Letter*")

Index